Why Be Moral?

American University Studies

Series V
Philosophy
Vol. 156

PETER LANG
New York • Washington, D.C./Baltimore • San Francisco
Bern • Frankfurt am Main • Berlin • Vienna • Paris

John van Ingen

Why Be Moral?

The Egoistic Challenge

PETER LANG
New York • Washington, D.C./Baltimore • San Francisco
Bern • Frankfurt am Main • Berlin • Vienna • Paris

Library of Congress Cataloging-in-Publication Data

Van Ingen, John Frederick.
    Why be moral?: the egoistic challenge / John van Ingen.
        p.   cm. — (American university studies. Series V, Philosophy:
    vol. 156)
    Includes bibliographical references and index.
    1. Egoism.   I. Title.   II. Series.
    BJ1474.V36   1994   171′.9—dc20   93-36873
    ISBN 0-8204-2357-2   CIP
    ISSN 0739-6392

Die Deutsche Bibliothek-CIP-Einheitsaufnahme

Van Ingen, John Frederick:
Why be moral?: The egoistic challenge / John Frederick van Ingen.
- New York; San Francisco; Bern; Baltimore; Frankfurt am Main; Berlin;
Wien; Paris: Lang, 1994
    (American university studies: Ser. 5, Philosophy; Vol. 156)
    ISBN 0-8204-2357-2
NE: American university studies / 05

The paper in this book meets the guidelines for permanence and durability of
the Committee on Production Guidelines for Book Longevity of the
Council on Library Resources.

To my Father and Mother,

Daniel K. and Virginia C. van Ingen,

who encouraged me to play as a child
and reach as a man.

Acknowledgments

Because this book began as a doctoral thesis, I owe my largest intellectual debts to members of my dissertation committee at the University of Chicago. I am grateful to the late Alan Donagan, who was initially on my committee, read several drafts of key chapters, and later wrote letters supporting the manuscript's publication. I thankfully acknowledge Ian Mueller, who added moral support at a decisive time, provided detailed comments on two early drafts, and was especially helpful in my adjusting to simpler and clearer language.

I am grateful to Christine Korsgaard for her key role in my chapter-by-chapter re-writing of the 1985-88 dissertation draft. At the time, her continued interest in my progress helped so much in building my confidence and my expectations. This moral support along wih her suggestions and criticisms on every chapter helped me make dramatic improvements in that draft. I am especially appreciative of her encouraging me to articulate and discuss tentative ideas and rough arguments before they had been thoroughly developed.

I owe a large debt to Alan Gewirth for his teaching, both about philosophical positions and about the evaluation of arguments. Alan was my thesis director and challenged me for years to improve my understanding of my project but especially the quality of my supporting arguments. I appreciate Alan's encouragement over the last few years to prepare my manuscript for publication. In particular, he encouraged me to emphasize for the reader the special *individual* character of my account of the egoist and how it differs from the usual discussions of ethical egoism in the literature. The first chapter and the beginning of the third reflect this suggestion.

The author gratefully acknowledges the following publishers: Prometheus Books for use of quotations from Kai Nielsen's 1989 book *Why be Moral?*; University of Calgary Press for use of quotes from Jesse Kalin's 1975 article "Two Kinds of Moral Reasoning: Ethical Egoism as a Moral Theory" from the Canadian Journal of Philosophy; selected quotes from Bernard William's 1973 book *Problems of the Self* are reprinted with permission of Cambridge University Press; use of quotations from R.M. Hare's 1963 book *Freedom and Reason* are used by permission of Oxford University Press.

I am thankful to the University of St. Thomas for supporting my most recent revisions. To the Committee on Faculty Development, to Philosophy Chair Richard Berquist, and especially to Academic Vice-President Ralph Pearson, I am grateful for their providing a grant for the summer of 1993 to free me from teaching so that I could focus exclusively on my final draft. Sue Moro did the book's formatting. Her amazing Macintosh expertise made me look good on paper, turning my crude word-processing into a finished product. My thanks to student Chelsea Doren for her help with some library research this fall. My thanks to Barbara Grudt for her careful proofreading of every page of the final draft.

My colleague Susan Krantz provided a careful set of comments, critical suggestions and language improvements for Chapters One, Two and Five. Her help was especially appreciated since Chapters One and Five are completely new chapters in this final draft.

I am fortunate to share an office with Harold Austin, a special friend and my mentor over the last five years. Harry read and marked up every chapter of the book, adding pages of suggestions, comments and criticism. Many improvements are due to his suggestions. But his biggest help was his encouragement to publish my work in the first place. Harry knows Plato. He understood right away my Glaucon-type project, both what I wanted to do and also the difficulty of articulating such an argument, not only because of its detail but especially because he understands that not everyone who has read Plato takes his amoral challenge seriously.

I am grateful to my mother, Virginia, for her steadfast support. Throughout work on this book, including during difficult periods of slow progress on early drafts, she was a constant source of inspiration, to buoy me up and encourage me on, often over plates of good food in her very special kitchen.

To my four children, Katherine, Jane, Scott and Dan, thanks for respecting the reason that Dad had to work on his book. May each of you enjoy the excitement and power of ideas and learn to defend the ones worth defending.

Most especially, I thank my wife, Maxine. I cannot underestimate her help. Maxine married me in the middle of the early revisions, before my most difficult and challenging drafts. She looked at the top of my head instead of my face. She quietly allowed me to focus. I could not have written *this* book without her.

Table of Contents

Why Be Moral?

Part I

Why Should I Be Moral?

Chapter One

Introductory Discussion

Since Callicles and Thrasymachus hurled amoral challenges from the pages of Plato's *Gorgias* and *Republic*, writers in ethics have offered their favorite accounts of morality and its justifications with the realization that an alternative to their best efforts remains, whether or not they judge that it merits any credence. This alternative position holds that morality and its conventions of thought and practice are of no account, the pablum of the naive, the compromising crutch of the weak—the position that asks and answers the question: Why take morality seriously?

This challenging question has been often articulated as "Why should I be moral?" as coined by Bradley in his famous essay of the same title.[1] The question in various forms has kept popping up in the philosophical literature over the last four decades, in spite of repeated attempts to put it to rest.[2] This book defends an interpretation of the "Why should I be moral?" question as being not only meaningful, but of fundamental practical importance, a question that drives to the heart of philosophic ethics.

My defense of an interpretation is modeled in key respects on Plato's amoral challenge in Book II of his *Republic*. The first similarity is that the interpretation which I develop and defend is of the form "Why should I be X *rather than* Y?" when Y is a competing way of life which offers a fundamental normative choice distinct from X. In the *Republic* Socrates is asked to make the case for a life of justice in reply to competing arguments that the unjust life is the better life. Brothers Glaucon and Adeimantus set Socrates up to confront the question "Why should I be just rather than unjust?" The interpretation which I will defend is "Why should I be moral rather than an amoral egoist?": Why should I be moral rather than a person who rejects morality and its conventions and at the same time systematically acts only for exclusively self-interested reasons?

Secondly, like Plato, I develop a strongest-case analysis of a normative alternative to the just or moral life. Glaucon and Adeimantus push arguments for being a systematically unjust person. My interpretation of "Why should I be moral?" makes use of a strongest-case analysis of the amoral egoist, a normative option to the moral life. To make this option an interesting one with empirical applicability, I have developed an account of personal egoism to team with a morality-rejecting amoralism, arriving at an agency of amoral personal egoism. I will argue that this position as I characterize it is at the same time an amoral challenge, internally consistent, and retaining what William Frankena has called the "spirit of egoism."

Philosophical discussions of universal or impersonal egoism offer theories about what everyone should do (each should further her own self-interest); one of the strengths of these theories is that they avoid some important consistency problems by being able to account for universalizability in language-use and reason-giving. However, by reason of their universal structure, these theories pay the heavy theoretical price of having no empirical applicability in the real world. The agency of universal egoism is only a creation of philosophers, a product of the seminar room. In short, no one who is a genuine egoist, exclusively self-interested, would offer a universal theory guiding others to do likewise. In Plato's language, anyone who takes seriously such a position, in the sense of prescribing it for oneself at the fundamental level, is a self-defeating bungler.

What I offer is an interpretation that is keyed around the normative option of the life of the amoral personal egoist, a strongest-case analysis of the combined positions of the amoralist and the egoist. Unlike the universal egoist, the personal egoist secretly plans to further her own interests regardless of all other people. If she becomes efficient enough at this, she can become, following Glaucon's model of the perfectly unjust man, a master of her craft who can expertly evaluate the consequences of her choices and even retrieve any false steps.

A note regarding my approach as author and the nature and extent of my defense of amoral egoism in this book: Like Glaucon, I judge the just (moral) life to be the better life. I do not advocate amoral egoism. I concur with Glaucon's disclaimer, "It isn't, Socrates, that I believe any of that myself,"[3] regarding the superiority of the systematically unjust life. In fact, I abhor the purely egoistic character and her systematic life of deceit. I defend amoral egoism through large sections of this book from objections and criticisms *not* because I believe the egoistic life should not be criticized or that it is above criticism, but simply to show that well-intentioned arguments have been ineffective because they have underestimated the potential sophistication and adaptability of the egoistic position. Friends of morality have not been well served by such arguments. Thus far, objections to the egoistic life have not been directed at the most vulnerable assumptions of the egoistic position since these have remained unscrutinized.

The egoistic life *should* be criticized, both in the sense of critically analyzing it and in arguing against it as a choice for young people. But it should be criticized as a strongest-case challenge, not as a weak and uninteresting shadow of the original. On this particular topic, straw-man arguments are not only logically inefficient but very funny on the street corner. Efficient criticism requires beginning with a strongest-case analysis of the kind of agent the egoist can be at the most interesting and challenging level.

I defend amoral egoism from unsuccessful arguments in order to separate conceptually the amoral egoistic challenge from the moral life. In short, I defend egoism in order to clarify morality as distinct from a potentially challenging alternative. In fact, I take this book to be the first in a series of projects to clarify morality and to engage in a defense of a certain account of morality. Like Glaucon, "I've yet to hear anyone defend justice (morality) in the way I want,"[4] which includes defending the moral life as distinct from the life of the egoistic parasite with which it can be confused both in theory and practice.

Egoism in any interesting form has been conceptually neglected. Of course, the serious egoistic practitioner would never provide scrutiny of her own position, much less publicly defend it. I take up this service for the above-stated methodological reason in the spirit of Plato's Glaucon. Rather than starting with the presumed requirements any ethical theory must meet, such as standard ethical language and reason-giving consistency requirements, and then fitting the egoistic position into this ethical model, I will cautiously proceed in a different way, well aware that, if I am not methodologically vigilant, I may lose the original concept of the serious, consistent and systematic life-long egoist, due to inattention to theoretical detail about this normative candidate. My method will be to start with this concept of the egoistic agent "as she is," what such a person would be like, and then try to figure out how such a person would think and act consistently. Through earlier drafts of this book, as I worked with objections to the very raising of the "Why should I be moral?" question and with the consistency problems for the egoist in the areas of language use and reason-giving, I realized that I needed to come up with novel uses of language and reason-giving in order for my description of the genuine egoist to both be internally consistent and retain the "spirit of egoism." I attempt to provide such in this book, especially in Chapters Six and Seven of Part III.

I do not assume that the egoist I describe can completely avoid all inconsistency, but I proceed under the assumption that the most interesting inconsistency problems for egoism arise in the thinking and living of a sophisticated egoistic agent; and only when one has delineated the strongest case of such an egoist, who designs her illocutionary language and communication practices in order to maintain an internal consistency in thought and practice, can one best see the fundamental and systematic problems, both theoretical and practical, that arise from being an normative agent of this kind.

The interesting kind of amoral egoist who challenges morality in the spirit of Plato cannot be a self-defeating creation of the seminar room with no empirical applicability. I will try to characterize what a real egoist is like. Only such a strong characterization gives interest and viability to the hard question "Why should I be moral?"

Notes

1   F. H. Bradley, "Why Should I Be Moral?" *Ethical Studies* (Selected Essays) (New York: Liberal Arts Press, 1951), p. 3.

2   Some have argued that the question is either a contradictory request or a tautological question, and therefore that any attempt to answer such a question is either futile or uninteresting. The following are some classic objections from the literature:

On the self-contradictory objection, see John Hospers, *Human Conduct: An Introduction to the Problems of Ethics* (New York: Harcourt, Brace & World, 1961), pp. 191-95.

On the tautological objection, see Stephen Toulmin, *An Examination of the Place of Reason in Ethics* (Cambridge: Cambridge University Press, 1964), pp. 160-65; and P. S. Wadia, "Why Should I Be Moral?" *Australasian Journal of Philosophy* 42 (1964): 216-26.

See also A. I. Melden, "Why Be Moral?" *The Journal of Philosophy* 45 (1948): 449-56. Melden does not put his objection in linguistic terms. He argues that the question "Why be moral?" is an impossible question to answer. Since only the commitment to morality itself can be a reason for being moral, to demand some other reason, where no other is possible, is due to a basic confusion. With the challenging amoralist we have *no theoretical issue*, but only a practical problem of how to handle her.

For a contrasting view on the importance of "Why should I be moral?" see Paul W. Taylor *Principles of Ethics: An Introduction* (Encino, Calif.: Dickenson Publishing Co., 1975), pp. 208-27. Taylor leaves discussion of this question until his concluding chapter which he entitles "The Ultimate Question."

Kai Nielsen has defended "Why should I be moral?" against many-sided criticism as a legitimate question. See especially "Is 'Why Should I Be Moral' an Absurdity?" *Australasian Journal of Philosophy* 36 (1958): 25-32; "Why Should I Be Moral?" in his *Why Be Moral?* (Buffalo, N.Y.: Prometheus Books, 1989), pp. 167-95; "Why Should I Be Moral?—Revisited" in *Why Be Moral?*, pp. 284-300; and "Point of Morality" in his *Reason and Practice: A Modern Introduction to Philosophy* (New York: Harper & Row, 1971), pp. 314-19.

Although my treatment of the question "Why should I be moral?" and my analysis of its proper resolution are very different from those of Kai Nielsen, I remain indebted to his defense of the meaningfulness of the question for stimulating the development of my thought.

3   Plato, *Republic*, trans. G. M. A. Grube, revised by C. D. C. Reeve (Indianapolis: Hackett Publishing Company, Inc., 1992), p. 34 (358c).

4   Ibid.

Chapter Two

A Viable Interpretation
with Classical Roots

In defending my interpretation of "Why should I be moral?" as both viable and interesting, I will interweave three elements of my argument. I will begin by laying out the question as cleanly as possible, using the necessary conceptual distinctions, to show how my interpretation is distinct from alternative versions with less merit. In so doing I will show that the viability and interest of the question depends on the existence of a genuine normative alternative to being moral. I will argue that such an alternative can be described, and described with the spirit of Glaucon's challenge.

The second element of the Chapter Two argument is the treatment of objections to the very raising of the question "Why should I be moral?" I consider three basic kinds of objections at that point in the presentation where their treatment can be most clearly handled. This handling of basic objections is a very important part of clarifying my interpretation because showing *how* my interpretation evades being dead-ended by conclusive objections not only exhibits its interest and viability but also shows that the competing alternatives of being moral and being amorally egoistic are genuine options of choice as Plato recognized.

Thirdly, I delve into a select group of ethical classics which contribute greatly to the clarification of the question. In the cases of Plato, Kant and Sidgwick, their contributions to my interpretation are so great that it is accurate to say that I have simply tapped selectively into the dialogue of their respective arguments and channeled what I found most promising in a special way.[1]

FIRST-PERSON SINGULAR QUESTION

I begin my clarification by attending to the 'I' in the question and note that "Why should I be moral?" is asked from a first-person singular point of view. This kind of question is distinct from its social cousin, "Why should we be moral?" or "Why should we have a common morality?"   This latter first-person plural question is often given a Hobbesian answer with the threat of the state of nature hovering in the background.   Kurt Baier in the *Moral Point of View* takes this tack.[2] Baier argues that we should be moral because to be moral is to act from superior reasons. Moral reasons are a superior kind of reason because following them is in the best interest of everyone alike, when compared with the state of nature alternative. "The very *raison d'etre* of a morality is to yield reasons which overrule the reasons of self-interest in those cases when everyone's following self-interest would be harmful to everyone."[3] From the "God's-eye point of view" or the "point of view of anyone," upon examination of the two alternative worlds, the moral world is "a better world."

One who raises the question at issue can grant all this, given the advantages of social stability and cooperation for all in a society in which a healthy common morality is in operation. However, the first-person questioner sees more than the above two alternatives. Part of what is at issue is, why take the "God's-eye" view or the "point of view of anyone" in the first place? The challenge of the amoral egoist reminds us that there is at least one more alternative. As a parasite in a community with a common morality and much goodwill, the amoral egoist can recognize and enjoy the social advantages of a system that he personally disavows. In fact, the amoralist may work publicly to support the strengthening of society's "moral fabric" so that his egoistic planning and decision-making can take place in a stable arena with predictable social advantages. To avoid confusion with its social cousin, the question can be rephrased in this way: Why should I be moral in a society with a relatively stable political and legal system, in which a large majority of the population not only respects the law but also holds similar versions of a conventional morality?   This question is sometimes called the free-rider problem: why not ride free? As my presentation unfolds, this rephrased first-person singular question is the question at issue.

FIRST OBJECTION: TAUTOLOGICAL QUESTION?

Before presenting my initial characterization of the alternatives of being an amoral egoist and being moral, I here consider the first of three basic objections to the very raising of the question "Why should I be moral?" Considering this objection will facilitate my presentation of these fundamental alternatives. The first objection in its various forms states that the question is a pointless pseudo question because it is tautologous, asking only for moral reasons for respecting moral reasons in the first place, such as "Why am I morally required to be moral?" Stephen Toulmin in his classic *Reason in Ethics* provides an interesting instance of this kind of objection:

> For let us consider what kind of answer they want when they ask,"Why ought one to do what is right?" There is no room within ethics for such a question. Ethical reasoning may be able to show why we ought to do this action as opposed to that, or advocate this social practice as opposed to that, but it is no help where there can be no choice. And their question does not present us with genuine alternatives at all. For, since the notions of "right" and of "obligation" originate in the same situations and serve similar purposes, it is a self-contradiction (taking "right" and "ought" in their simplest senses) to suggest that we "ought" to do anything but what is "right." This suggestion is as unintelligible as the suggestion that some emerald objects might not be green, and the philosopher's question is on a level with the question, "Why are all scarlet things red? ... if those that call for a "justification" of ethics want "the case for morality," as opposed to "the case for expediency," etc., then they are giving philosophy a job which is not its own. To show that you ought to choose certain actions is one thing; to make you *want to do* what you ought to do is another, and not a philosopher's task.[4]

Toulmin goes on to explain that, although there is no literal sense to a question such as "Why should I be moral?", the question is a "limiting question" which "... comes alive again as soon as one takes it 'spiritually,' as a religious question";[5] and as such the question serves the psychological function of helping us to accept the world, in particular to help us want to do what is morally right.

This objection makes a strong case only if one interprets the "why should I" as exclusively a question about moral requirements within the framework of morality. However, this exclusive, inside-morality interpretation is just not interesting and does not provide a challenge in the spirit of Plato. What is challenging is a question that starts in the following way: Given the present status of the logic of moral language and reasoning, with all the requirements of morality defined within its framework and limits, and given the possibility of an amoralist who may adopt her own special "logic" and reasoning, what reason is there for me to accept one of these types of agency, language and all, rather than another? Part of the challenge is that the thinking and language within either framework does not decide the question, for part of the question involves asking why take either one of these positions and all their habits of thought and practice seriously in the first place, in the sense of prescribing them for oneself as definitive of one's most basic normative commitments?

I will discuss further in Chapter Seven whether my interpreted question lies within or without the proper boundaries of philosophic ethics. It is interesting to note that the above question fails to meet one of Toulmin's criteria for a limiting question, that a limiting question does not present us with a "genuine alternative to choose between." In fact, this very point lies at the heart of my argument: It is this genuine alternative of fundamental normative options, being amorally egoistic or being moral, which gives credence to my claim that "Why should I be moral?" has considerable philosophic interest.

AMORAL OPTION

My initial characterization of the fundamental normative alternative begins with a description of the amoral egoist. An amoral person is one who is *without morality* in thought and practice. An amoralist with some knowledge of human behavior and some experience in human relations will not deliberately avoid all actions required by moral practices, nor will she transgress all moral prohibitions. In fact, as I will emphasize in the chapters ahead, the clever amoral egoist will seek the social advantages of acting in accordance with moral practices for the most part, while maximizing the payoff of each carefully planned deviation. The amoralist does not act in accord with moral practices just *because morality requires.* Morality is rejected by the amoralist as the supremely authoritative practical guide, indeed, as any real guide at all. Not only does the amoralist deny (at least to herself) that she has any obligations or duties to others, the amoralist does not share at all what many persons strongly hold: That a common set of principles about right and wrong behavior applies to oneself *and others*, and as such provides a common supremely authoritative guide for human action.

The amoralist's rejection of morality affects her use and understanding of normative language. She disavows, at least privately, any supremely authoritative, non-hypothetical use of terms such as "right" or "ought" as applicable to herself and others in a common way. For example, the consistent amoralist does not prescribe in a serious way judgments such as "Murder for personal gain is wrong" or "Providing food for one's children is right." If the amoralist were to prescribe such judgments, she would be participating in a non-amoralist practice. However, the use of a means-end hypothetical, such as "If I want to get to the APA meeting, I ought to steal money for plane fare," is not problematic for the amoralist because it does not imply a commitment to a common supremely authoritative system of right and wrong. The hypothetical merely implies the use of the practice of making means-end efficiency claims. The further questions are left open, such as, to what normative system does she commit herself and with which illocutionary acts and normative terms does she articulate her fundamental normative prescription.[6]

Similarly, if others use normative terms in a non-hypothetical, supremely authoritative way, such as "Emil Amoralist ought to clean up the environment," the amoralist denies that such judgments meaningfully apply to her. Of course, the amoralist is *not* denying any of the following: (1) that people in fact are now applying, and do apply in general, such normative terms to her (and others); (2) that such judgments are in fact taken to have meaning by those participants within the practice of morality; and even (3) that people sometimes intend to apply meaningfully such terms to outsiders like Emil Amoralist. However, insofar as she rejects the whole practice of morality, such second- or third-person judgments by others about herself (or about groups of people that include herself), do not from the amoralist's point of view successfully apply with meaning to her. Like a communication from a transmitter that is not received by a transmitter-designated receiver, the intended "meaningful application" does not go through. While the amoralist admits that moral terms are taken mistakenly by moralists to have powerful meanings within the moral practice, she simply rejects the assumption that such terms meaningfully apply to her on the outside. Of course, independent of the question of the "origin" of morality or its *raison d'etre*, the amoralist assumes this practice of morality is, for her, an optional practice that she is free to accept or reject.

At this point in my initial characterization of the amoral egoist, it is important to note that the above amoralist position is entirely negative. To hold that one's most basic practical principle and related practices of thought and action are void of a certain content says nothing definite about what content is left. Plato's Thrasymachus may value only the exercise of power; another amoralist may hold that aesthetic experiences of a certain kind must be maximized at any price.

AMORALIST WHO IS AN EGOIST

The kind of amoralist who plays the central character in this book is the amoralist who holds a distinctive procedural position as to how to order one's normative life. By one's normative life, I here simply mean one's practical life (what to do), including some rules for guiding what one does and some principles for prioritizing judgments, rules and the maintenance program for one's habits. The morality-rejecting amoralist who is also an egoist goes on to affirm as her most basic practical principle that principle of choice which gives exclusive priority to her own wants in interpersonal transactions. The amoral egoist holds, as her orientation to all of life's choices, that she ought to seek her own wants exclusively and disregard the wants of all others, unless the satisfaction of the want of another is calculated to satisfy a prioritized want of her own. Accordingly, such an egoist ultimately evaluates in a hierarchical manner all her individual judgments, as well as rules and practices she either develops or takes advantage of, on the basis of her fundamental prescriptive principle: "I ought to seek the satisfaction of my own wants exclusively and disregard the wants of all other persons, except when attending to others' wants is instrumentally helpful in my solitary pursuit." The amoral egoist fully prescribes and endorses a special group of first-person judgments that are based upon her fundamental egoistic principle and as such systematically apply to herself alone. Such a system calls for developing special egoistic rules, character traits and habits to facilitate successful action within the egoistic program.

The *role of other persons* is unique in the amoral egoist's account. Instead of sharing with others the roles of evaluator and respected agent, in a group bound together under a common system of evaluation, the amoral egoist looks at other persons as simply obstacles or resources, tethered to her solitary program only by its instrumental applications. In light of the amoral egoist's perception of all other people as but hindrances to her plans or as tools in bringing them about, one can reformulate her fundamental egoistic prescription in the form of a fundamental imperative, that applies by systematic stipulation to one person only: "Treat all of humanity, except in my own person, always as a means only, and never as an end as I treat myself."

MORAL AGENT DEFINED

Having completed my initial characterization of one of the two options of that genuine normative alternative central to my interpretation, I turn now to a working definition of "being moral." A human agent is "moral," if and only if that agent includes within her most basic practical principles the stipulation that some possible choices in the pursuit of her wants are absolutely ruled out simply because the consequences of such choices conflict in relevant ways with the welfare of some *other* persons. The moral agent refuses to treat the interests of others simply as data in exclusively self-interested calculations. With the moral agent, so defined, we have a concept of practical correctness which is distinct from and not reducible to simple adherence to a single person's want-satisfaction efficiency.

Notice that my use of "moral" here is a minimal notion with broad application, designed to capture a large class of agents and basic principles that share a common feature. This broader use of "moral" is distinct from those senses of the term opposed to "immoral"; for the term "moral" here used is neutral with respect to the further question of the morally *best* agent, principle, or theory. So that in this minimal sense of "moral," a Nazi nationalist or a godfather of a criminal organization, as well as Christians, Utilitarians, etc., would be termed moral agents, as long as the welfare of *some* other people, such as fellow Nazis or family members, is built into the agents' practical principles at the most basic level. Hence, while such Nazis or underworld figures are roundly judged to be immoral in their thoughts and actions for not meeting *the* standards of moral decency, as viewed from many different accounts of what is *the best* moral principle or theory, such persons may be correctly described as moral agents in this minimal sense, and not amoral egoists. Unless explicitly stated otherwise, the reader can assume that all uses of "moral" throughout the book will be in this minimal sense.

THE FUNDAMENTAL ALTERNATIVE

Given this definition of "moral," notice the conceptual relationship between the amoral egoist and the moral agent as defined above; one cannot be both. Also one cannot be neither an amoral egoist nor a moral agent, as long as one reaches a minimal level of reflection and confronts the question, what to do about others in guiding and planning one's practical life. So, if one is not an amoral egoist, one is a moral agent in the above minimal sense; and if one is not a moral agent, then one is an amoral egoist. Thus understood, the question "Why should I be moral?" asks "Why should I be a non-egoist?" or, more accurately,"Why should I be moral at all, rather than an amoral egoist?"

On first face "Why should I be moral rather than an amoral egoist?" appears to be a much less ambitious question than "Why should I live in accord with the morally best principle rather than be an amoral egoist?" However, the challenge of the former question is itself considerable if one takes the amoral egoist option seriously and treats it as a strongest case challenge. Furthermore, this less specific and less idealistic question has a methodological advantage by reason of its limitations, not shared by the question "Why should I be moral in the sense of the morally best?" To raise the question "Why should I be moral?" in my minimal sense is to seek a reason for accepting *any* non-egoistic morality over the amoral egoistic alternative, to seek to evaluate thereby the relative advantages, intellectual and practical, for accepting non-egoism over amoral egoism.

The focus of this book is on the importantly overlooked differences between amoral egoism and all other normative alternatives. Amoral egoism has benefited considerably from a form of conceptual neglect. When the morally best ethical theory is at issue, it is easy for philosophers to gravitate toward the tough intellectual infighting regarding the argumentative weaknesses of each candidate vying to be considered the best account of morality. Meanwhile, egoism with its initial allurement intact avoids the same scrutiny demanded of non-egoistic ethical theories. My interpretation "Why should I be moral rather than an amoral egoist?" is designed to force the amoral egoist to play "hard ball" as well, and thereby to subject the amoral egoist to much needed scrutiny and evaluation right alongside its normative competitors.

PLATO'S AMORAL CHALLENGE

With the initial characterization of my interpretation in place, I turn again to Plato's amoral challenge from the *Republic*. In discussing Plato's contribution, I point out six features of Plato's amoral challenge which are also features of my interpretation of "Why should I be moral?" The similarities to Plato's account will clarify my interpretation by exhibiting what is fundamentally at stake in the normative option of being an amoral egoist versus being a moral agent.

The *first feature* of Plato's challenge to emphasize is that for Plato a *genuine normative alternative* is at the heart of the arguments for and against justice in the *Republic*. This alternative is between being just and being unjust while deceitfully appearing to be just for its social advantages. Plato takes seriously as a live option the *systematically* unjust man who *systematically* schemes not to pay the price for his injustice. The justice question is not treated as merely academic; Thrasymachus is not written off as failing to use language correctly or because of an out-moded methodology; two brothers who are against the unjust life push the case for injustice "with all the force (they) can muster." The arguments come to life for Plato because the option is a real one.

The *second feature* of Plato's challenge is that the alternative of being just versus being unjust is a question about *a way of life*, whose answer completely affects every aspect of one's normative life. The issue here is far removed from and more basic than any individual choice regarding whether to cheat or to be unfair in a given situation.[7] These specific case questions can be answered in part by replies such as "I do not do that," "I can pull it off without detection," or "That is against standard XYZ." But for more complete answers, more fundamental questions are relevant, such as "Should I develop a personal character and corresponding habits such that choices of a certain sort are automatically handled in ways A and B?"; or "Should I be the sort of person whose only judgmental criterion regarding questions about cheating or lying is whether I will be caught and receive X and Y punishments?"; or "Should I be the sort of person who values a given standard as supremely authoritative, or should I rather treat all such standards as expedient rules of thumb in pursuing all that I can get?" For Plato, the first question in order of normative importance is not a question about whether or not to scheme a certain way in situation X, but about whether I should be a schemer at all. Plato's treatment of the justice question is always as a question about a fundamental way of life, such as when he speaks of the young person's questioning the "... sort of person he should be and ... how best to travel the road of life?"[8]

A *third feature*, related to the second, is that for Plato this fundamental way of life question is of fundamental *practical importance*. In Book I on the question of whether the life of justice is the better and happier life, Plato's Socrates says, "... we must look into it further, since the argument concerns no ordinary topic but the way we ought to live."[9]

In the *Gorgias* in discussing Callicles' account of "natural justice," Socrates states:

> And of all inquiries, Callicles, the noblest is that which concerns the very matter with which you have reproached me—namely, what a man should be, and what he should practice and to what extent, both when older and when young.[10]

Again Plato emphasizes how far reaching this fundamental question can be through the words of Adeimantus:

> ... (A young person) would surely ask himself Pindar's question, "Should I by justice or by crooked deceit scale this high wall and live my life guarded and secure?"[11]

Francis M. Cornford translates Pindar's famous question as follows, more expicitly emphasizing its long-range importance:

> In all likelihood [a young man] would ask himself, in Pindar's words: "Will the way of right or the by-paths of deceit lead me to the higher fortress," where I may entrench myself for the rest of my life?[12]

The fourth and fifth features of Plato's challenge are interestingly related. The *fourth feature* is that the question of a life of justice or a life of injustice is for *every* person a *matter of individual choice*. A person may choose at a level of minimal reflection to let another person, or an institution, tell him how to live, but it is his choice[13] at least in the sense that he has to live with the option he goes with.

> Now, it seems that it is here, Glaucon, that a human being faces the greatest danger of all. And because of this, each of us must neglect all

other subjects and be most concerned to seek out and learn those that will enable him to distinguish the good life from the bad ... from all this he will be able, by considering the nature of the soul, to reason out which life is better and which worse and to choose accordingly, calling a life worse if it leads the soul to become more unjust, better if it leads the soul to become more just, and ignoring everything else: We have seen that this is the best way to choose, whether in life or death.[14]

The related *fifth feature* of Plato's amoral challenge is one about methodology and the limits of philosophic argument. For Plato, each *individual choice is made within and not beyond the effective reach of philosophic critique*. Plato does *not* run all practical questions down to this ultimate form of justice versus injustice, then close the door on the province of philosophic argument[15] and embrace a relativism at the fundamental level. No character in Plato's challenge claims that any one person's choice is by definition or by methodological stipulation as good as any other person's. As Plato makes his argumentative case for the life of justice, the question of truth, and who is naive and who is ignorant, is still at stake.

Paul W. Taylor takes an interestingly contrasting view in his book *Principles of Ethics: An Introduction*. On his book's last three pages, Taylor raises the question, whether a person's "ultimate commitment" to the supremacy of moral principles over self-interest is an arbitrary decision, like the tossing of a coin? Taylor answers that "As an ultimate choice it can be called extrarational, beyond reason, neither rational nor irrational."[16] Taylor goes on to discuss the case of a person's making an ultimate choice to destroy someone else's capacity for making ultimate choices. If such a person says "Why should I care?" whether others are able to seek and find an answer to the "ultimate question," Taylor says,

There are no reasons that can be given which provide an answer to this question. He must decide for himself what he is to care about in his life. The only thing that can be done is to point out to him that this is a decision of a fundamental kind. It is the decision to be a certain sort of person. Can he face himself openly and unevasively and still decide not to respect the autonomy of others, having clearly before his mind the full meaning of such a choice? If he can, then he has determined what conception of human shall be exemplified in his life and this is all one can say about this decision. No argument can be given to show that his decision is irrational or that it is based on false assumptions ... .

> Commitment to moral principles, then, is finally a matter of one's
> will, not of one's reason ... . Reason alone cannot tell us what choice
> to make. We must not expect, therefore, that someone might provide us
> with an argument showing which alternative ought to be chosen. There
> is simply no way to evade the responsibility—a responsibility that rests
> upon each of us alone—for defining our own selves.[17]

Plato, of course, agrees with Taylor that each of us has the
responsibility to define her fundamental normative person. But
the most basic difference between Plato and Taylor involves *what
is at stake* when each person defines her person. Of course, Plato
reminds us that the consequences for personal happiness are tied
tightly to the "fortress" in which each one of us ultimately decides
to entrench herself. But such choices involve the risk not only of
personal peril and unhappiness, but for Plato there is also the risk
of ultimately being a fool or ignorant. As evidenced by his use of
the characters Glaucon and Adeimantus, for Plato the amoral
challenge consists of much more than how to handle
philosophically an unsettling Thrasymachus with his new uses for
normative terms. At bottom, the amoral challenge is present to
any person who, no matter how confusedly, sees the practical
alternative of the unjust life of deceit. It is significant that where
Taylor ends his book, with nothing more to share, at the point of
the ultimate question, where each of us must at bottom define
herself, Plato begins his *Republic* with the reality of the amoral
normative alternative. From there, Plato goes on to argue that the
case for justice is the stronger, never once considering abandoning
the presumption that discourse and argument are necessary, if not
sufficient, for the twofold task at hand: to show which choice
makes one happier and to show which choice exhibits knowledge
and which one ignorance. For Plato, the knowledge of reality
accurately described, including a genuine understanding of the
consequences of a life of injustice, is practically necessary for
avoiding the costs of ignorance.

The key question for Taylor is: When does one have before
one's mind the "full meaning" of one's choice? If part of one's
assumptions or presumptions that give full meaning to one's
choice are based upon questionable or mistaken premises, there is
much work for us Plato-inspired philosophers, who see life not
only as a defining process with tremendous personal risk, but also
as a continual process of sharing in the examination of the

possibilty of choosing from a perspective of knowledge or ignorance.

The *sixth feature* of Plato's amoral challenge is that *the amoral alternative is not for everyone* but only those of "superior powers" of thought and courage. Adeimantus points out that, as a matter of fact, given men's motives, most people are not virtuous of their own unforced choice,

> ... apart from someone of godlike character who is disgusted by injustice or one who has gained knowledge and avoids injustice for that reason, no one is just willingly. Through cowardice or old age or some other weakness, people do indeed object to injustice. But it's obvious that they do so only because they lack the power to do injustice, for the first of them to acquire it is the first to do as much injustice as he can.[18]

In discussing "Why should I be moral?" in his book *Moral Thinking*, R.M. Hare offers a thought experiment in which one is deciding how to bring up a child in such a way that one "had only the child's interests at heart."[19] This way of looking at the problem, according to Hare, provides a "modest" but adequate defense of morality. At bottom, Hare's argument rests on empirical claims that it would be very difficult to be the amoral egoist, or to teach a child to be one. Hare pushes the question to the interesting point where he asks, why not bring up the child to conform for the most part to the accepted moral practices to remain in good social standing, but to "transgress them cynically" when he can escape detection and/or retribution, all the while leaving out any teaching of the disposition to feel shame or guilt at transgression? Hare answers,

> Here again we trespass on the empirical; but has not the difficulty of bringing this off been underrated? It is a question of what dispositions are co-viable. My guess is that the safest and best way of bringing up our child is to implant in him, if one can, a good set of moral principles plus the feelings that go with them, the feelings being strong enough to secure observance of the principles in all ordinary cases ...[20]

But Hare's modest defense of morality misses completely the amoralist challenge as classically understood. Hare's empirical appeal to the "safest way ... in ordinary cases" reads like a union rule defined to cover all the workers, even the least capable. But Plato's amoralist challenge reads: If I am of superior ability of mind and spirit, then why should I live a life of justice, rather than a life of injustice in which I can deceitfully and cleverly save appearances? As Adeimantus notes, "'But surely,' someone will object, 'it isn't easy for vice to remain always hidden.' We'll reply that nothing great is easy."[21] The amoral option is not for everyone.

In summary, my interpretation of "Why should I be moral?" like Plato's amoral challenge[22] is a far-reaching practical question about a fundamental choice between two systematically distinct normative alternatives involving distinct ways of living and distinct ways of treating other persons. Like Plato's question, this fundamental and individual choice is made within and not beyond the reach of philosophic critique and realistically is not open to everyone alike, since the successful amoral egoist like Plato's perfectly unjust man requires superior abilities in intelligence and courage. I present these comparative claims here in Chapter Two for clarification purposes; argumentative support for these claims will be given throughout the book as I add to my articulation of the fundamental choice by adding to the characterization of the amoral egoistic option.

KANT'S PRACTICAL CONFLICT

Immanuel Kant's contributions to the question "Why should I be moral rather than amorally egoistic?" arise from his discussions of the practical conflict between prudence and morality. My discussion of Kant will have two stages. First of all, I will discuss why Kant never presents the completely amoral rebel as a serious alternative. Secondly, I will consider the second and third kinds of basic objection that can be made to the question and I will discuss how each objection is based upon a Kantian theme.

Kant writes in his *Critique of Practical Reason* that there is practical conflict within every human person between the maxims of self-love or prudence on the one hand and the law of morality on the other. The former advises one hypothetically (If I want X, then I ought to do Y) and the latter commands one categorically.

> When one's own happiness is made the determining ground of the will, the result is the direct opposite of the principle of morality ... . This conflict is not, however, merely logical ... it is rather a practical conflict ... .[23]

However, for Kant, the amoral alternative does not arise as a live option of systematically resolving one's practical conflict between prudence and morality:

> Man (even the most wicked) does not, under any maxim whatsoever, repudiate the moral law in the manner of a rebel (renouncing obedience to it). The law, rather, forces itself upon him irresistibly by virtue of his moral predisposition: and were no other incentive working in opposition, he would adapt the law into his supreme maxim as the sufficient determining ground of his will; that is, he would be morally good. [24]

The moral law, according to Kant is a "fact of reason" (pure reason thereby becoming by itself practical), whose voice to the will is "... so distinct, so irrepressible, and so clearly audible to even the commonest man ... ."[25] The systematic alternatives for resolving this practical conflict are therefore both defined in moral terms: the morally good and the morally evil man.

> Hence the distinction between a good man and one who is evil cannot lie in the differences between the incentives ... but rather must depend upon subordination (the form of the maxim), i.e., which of the two incentives he makes the condition of the other. Consequently man (even the best) is evil only in that he reverses the moral order of the incentives when he adopts them into his maxim ... he makes the incentive of self-love and its inclinations the condition of obedience to the moral law ... .[26]

SECOND OBJECTION: SELF-CONTRADICTORY REQUEST?

Both the second and third basic objections to the question "Why should I be moral?" can now be most effectively handled. Both objections are raised from the point of view of morality or from within the framework of morality. Also, in both objections the "Why should" part of the question is interpreted as a request for an exclusively prudential explanation. So interpreted, the question becomes "Why is it in my best interest to be moral?" The second basic objection to the question, based on this self-interested interpretation, is that such a question is a self-contradictory request that rests on a conceptual confusion. John Hospers notes that people do sometimes make such self-contradictory requests and are disappointed when their questions cannot be answered, but that they are disappointed is no more surprising than the failure of one who searches for square circles. "Of course it is impossible to give him a reason in accordance with his interest for acting contrary to his interest."[27]

The conceptual distinction upon which this objection is based is certainly a Kantian point. Taking a moral point of view involves recognizing that one is *obliged* to do certain things irrespective of whether one wants to so act. Self-interested reasons provide motives why we may also *want* to do such morally required acts, by explaining their role as means to ends that we want; but such motives and their corresponding "hypothetical imperatives" are conceptually distinct from obligations, for it is precisely the task of obligations to bind one in spite of one's inclinations. To ask why it is in one's self-interest to be moral is to ask the moral law with its categorical requirements to be the consequent in a hypothetical imperative.

> The principle of personal happiness ... contributes nothing whatever towards establishing morality, since making a man happy is quite different from making him good and making him prudent or astute in seeking his advantage quite different form making him virtuous ... .[28]

Furthermore, on Kant's view, the ability to make this distinction between morality's requirements and self-interest is not due to sophisticated philosophical finesse: "So distinct and sharp are the boundaries between morality and self-love that even the commonest eye cannot fail to distinguish whether a thing belongs to the one or the other."[29]

One might reply to this second objection, the objection that such a question is a contradictory request based on conceptual confusion, by denying that all interpretations of "Why is it in my self-interest not to act in my self-interest?" are self-contradictory. For example, the question "Why is it prudent to act for reasons that are not in my *immediate* self-interest?" is not contradictory. In fact, I will argue in Chapter Three that the personal egoist will have self-interested reasons to suspend egoistic calculation in special situations, as a rule egoist. Similarly, Joseph Butler warns us that, if one's general desire for happiness is so strong that it crowds out one's particular natural desires, and therefore the sources of one's satisfactions, then such an "... immoderate self-love does very ill consult its own interest ... ."[30] Accordingly, one can ask with no contradiction a question such as: Why is it in my self-interest to free my forward-looking calculations from short-sighted preoccupation with my satisfaction efficiency? However, this kind of reply to the second objection does not silence the objection, but only requires the objector to qualify his question more carefully: Why is it in my self-interest to act for reasons that are not in my long-range interest, nor *indirectly* based on my self-interest at all? The answer can only be that to do so is *not* in my interest, that it does not make sense to ask such a question, that it is a self-contradictory question when stated in this more complete way.

H. A. Prichard follows Kant on the clear-cut distinction between prudence and morality. Prichard criticizes Plato for buying the presupposition of the Sophists, that it is personal profitability that really makes an action just. Prichard writes,

> What Plato should have said to the Sophists is: ... You do nothing whatever to show that [convictions about what actions are right] are false by urging that the actions in question are disadvantageous; and I should do nothing to show that they are true, if I were to show that these actions are after all advantageous. Your real mistake lies in presupposing throughout that advantageousness is what renders an action a duty.[31]

But if Plato gave too much away to the Sophists at the start due to not articulating the crucial distinction between prudence and moral rightness, could not Glaucon and Adeimantus just include Prichard's whole account of intuiting one's moral obligations in their challenge of justice? A dialogue based upon practical alternatives with distinct normative commitments and thinking still remains. Glaucon can claim that Prichard's moral thinking (the whole theoretical package and practice) "rests on a mistake"—it is naive and personally foolish to hold. The question he still asks is why should he think as a moral agent at all rather than as an amoral egoist?

The next question is how Kant and Prichard can reply to Glaucon's challenge, which brings me to the third basic objection. I turn to consideration of objection three before completing the discussion of objection two because a complete reply to both objections requires attending to the same interpretive presuppositions.

THIRD OBJECTION: INDICATES CORRUPT MIND?

Objection three charges that to ask a question such as "Why should I be moral?" is indicative of a corrupt mind. Kant and Prichard could reply, to Glaucon's charge that Kant and Prichard are naive and foolish, that Plato's challenge, whether articulated with or without conceptual confusion about prudence and justice, is simply indicative of a morally corrupt mind.

F. H. Bradley follows Kant on this third kind of objection. In his essay, "Why Should I Be Moral?" Bradley argues that this strange question is based on the dogma that virtue is only good as a means, and "that (moral) consciousness, when unwarped by selfishness and not blinded by sophistry, is convinced that to ask for the Why? is simple immorality ... ."[32] Also, Bradley shares with Kant a concern that this assumption that virtue is only good as a means, that is at the bottom of such a corrupt mind, can be destructive of morality, conceptually dissolving morality in her true form into something much less:

> For morality ... teaches us that, if we look on her only as good for something else, we never in that case have seen her at all ... . Degrade her, and she disappears; and to keep her, we must love and not merely use her.[33]

SAVING THE QUESTION: WHY SHOULD I BE MORAL RATHER AN AMORAL EGOIST?

The keys to evaluating both objections two and three are (a) the presumptive interpretation of the "Why should I" part of the question and (b) the evaluative framework from which the objections are delivered. Both objections presume that "Why should I" is asking an exclusively prudential question: "Why is it in my self-interest (to be moral)?" Also both objections presume a distinct concept of morality as the appropriate evaluative standard. Given both assumptions, the objections are conclusive. However, are not the assumptions themselves at issue in asking "Why should I be moral?" I argue affirmatively that assumptions regarding interpretation and evaluation standpoints are themselves part of what is at issue in the question. In fact, it is because these assumptions themselves are at issue that the question does not dead-end, but rather a genuine practical alternative at the fundamental level can be articulated.

In my question "Why should I be moral rather than an amoral egoist?" the fundamental normative alternative between being moral and being amorally egoistic is the live option. So interpreted, the question "Why should I be moral?" is neither an *exclusively* moral question nor an *exclusively* prudential question about being moral. As we learned from objection one, to ask the exclusively moral question "Why am I morally required to be moral?" is to ask a pointless tautologous question. And as we learned from objections two and three, to ask "Why is it prudent to be moral?" can be a contradictory request and can indicate one's attitude toward morality. But to ask "Why should I be moral rather than an amoral egoist?" is to ask about the evaluative standpoints themselves: to pit the amorally egoistic standpoint against all others, with no presumption about which questions are the only possible or the only permissible questions, with no presumption about the only way to interpret "should," with no presumption about *the* only fundamental evaluative standard. The presumptions of themselves not only do not decide the fundamental question at this level, but neither do they dead-end nor quiet the question. Charges from the moral community that the amoral egoist is corrupt and conceptually confused about his obligations carry no weight for the amoralist who is a "master of his craft." Similarly, if the amoral egoist were short-sighted or undisciplined enough to charge the moralists with sheer personal ignorance, such a comparative knowledge claim from such an evaluative framework, if properly understood, may elicit a reply such as "Consider the source … ." But, is not this what we would expect in the arena of action—where the normative sides are drawn?

SIDGWICK'S QUESTION

The idea of different fundamental practical alternatives with different fundamental evaluative standards is not something with which Henry Sidgwick would be at all uncomfortable. Sidgwick bases the very plan of his book *The Methods of Ethics* on his conviction that the ordinary man implicitly holds that there are different views of the "ultimate reasonableness of conduct." According to Sidgwick, the fact that "the unphilosophic man" may hold a confused combination of ultimate practical principles at once is the only sufficient explanation for a privately recurring phenomenon in normative discourse. This persistently recurring phenomenon is that people "widely and continually" ask the question, "Why should I do what I see to be right?"

> For if there are different views of the ultimate reasonableness of conduct, implicit in the thought of ordinary men, though not brought into clear relation to each other—it is easy to see that any single answer to the question 'why' will not be completely satisfactory, as it will be

given only from one of these points of view, and will always have room to ask the question from some other.[34]

Therefore, a question such as "Why should I be moral?" is continually raised, according to Sidgwick, because the confused ordinary person, who combines a number of different ultimate principles in his thought, can continually jump from one ultimate explanation to another, repeatedly questioning each "ultimately reasonable" explanation in light of another.

One difficulty with Sidgwick's interesting explanation is that it does not seem to explain why philosophers, who pride themselves in spotting and rooting out inconsistencies, have continued to raise a question such as "Why should I be moral?" Also there is an important type of situation in which one can meaningfully ask the question, but Sidgwick's explanation cannot account for such cases. Imagine a single determined person who is not content to be like Sidgwick's ordinary person, who confusedly holds to multiple ultimate principles; rather this person is in search of a single ultimate principle to which to commit his life. Such a person can still meaningfully ask "Why should I be moral?" or "Why should I do what I see to be right?"

EXPLAINING THE PERSISTING QUESTION

At bottom the persisting question as applied to philosophers and non-philosophers alike leads back to the question of fundamental normative alternatives. The reason why it is possible that Sidgwick's ordinary man can confusedly hold to two ultimate principles of evaluation is the same reason why one of two conceptually consistent persons may be an amoral egoist while the other holds a moral point of view. The common reason is that being moral and being amorally egoistic present two different fundamental alternatives for practical acceptance. The question persists because the fundamental practical alternative persists, reflective people in each generation can raise again the basic practical question, "Why should I be moral rather than an amoral egoist?"

Sidgwick's object in *The Methods of Ethics,*

> ... is to expound as clearly and as fully as my limits will allow the different methods of Ethics that I find implicit in our common moral reasoning; to point out their mutual relations; and where they seem to conflict, to define the issue as much as possible.[35]

In his final chapter Sidgwick concludes his examination of the relation between the egoistic method and the utilitarian method, concerned that Common Sense suggests, "... a harmony between the maxim of Prudence and the maxim of Rational Benevolence must be somehow demonstrated, if morality is to be made completely rational."[36] Sidgwick concludes that we must "... admit an ultimate and fundamental contradiction in our apparent intuitions of what is Reasonable in conduct ...," unless the reconciliation of duty (or virtue) and self-interest can be proved or postulated.[37] He argues that the necessary connection cannot be proven either on empirical grounds or by mere reflective intuition; but that our Practical Reason can attain complete synthesis only by postulating such a connection or by postulating the existence of God who will bring about such a reconciliation through rewards and punishments.

I summarize Sidgwick's argument as it touches on self-interest and duty, not to evaluate his argument which is beyond my purposes, but to emphasize the contrast between his objective and mine. In his critical exposition of the alternative methods, including the egoistic method, Sidgwick starts with the variously confused practical reasonings of *ordinary* men. The product of his careful examination is a clarified account of a *common morality* that *we* share.[38]

In pushing the question "Why should I be moral rather than amorally egoistic?" I focus on that fundamental option whose egoistic agency seeks no serious share in a common morality. Understanding the amorally egoistic agent requires no less than a thorough examination of a singular method of egoism[39] without any distraction from or confusion with the intuitions, language and common reasoning that characterize all of us, who like Sidgwick, are not amoral egoists. Rather than attending to the question of whether an egoistic method can be synthesized with our other shared methods, I focus all consistency questions on the amoral egoist's agency itself, to see how her unique method, which she shares with no other person, can be applied in a world of people who use normative methods and share concepts and commitments that the amoral egoist rejects.

In summary, I have presented the initial clarification and argument for a viable and interesting interpretation of the question "Why should I be moral?" With the help of the thought of Plato,

Kant, and Sidgwick, I have defended the question "Why should I be moral rather than an amoral egoist?" against three fundamental objections: that such a question is pointlessly tautologous, that it is self-contradictory because it is based upon a conceptual confusion, and that it is indicative of a corrupt mind. My interpretation is viable insofar as it does not dead-end in the grasp of a conclusive objection. The interpretation is interesting insofar as it captures the amoralist's challenge in the spirit of Plato's Glaucon. And the key to its viability and interest is found in the genuine fundamental normative alternatives, being moral or being amorally egoistic. There is much to articulate further and run under consistency tests before attempting to sketch an answer. But at this point I concur with Sidgwick that in ethics, as in other disciplines, "... it [is] an advantage to draw as distinct a line as possible between the known and the unknown; as the clear indication of an unsolved problem is at any rate a step to its solution."[40]

Notes

[1] In this chapter and in later chapters I will also draw upon the thought of Plato or Kant, for example, at various points in the presentation not primarily to signal their substantive contribution to my thought or their role in providing an intellectual context, but simply to bring life to my argument because of the efficiency and force of their own presentations.

[2] Kurt Baier, *The Moral Point of View: A Rational Basis of Ethics*, abridged ed. (New York: Random House, 1965), see Chaps. 5 and 7.

[3] Ibid., p. 150.

[4] Toulmin, *Reason in Ethics*, pp. 162-63.

[5] Ibid., p. 218.

[6] I have purposely omitted in this initial clarification of the amoral egoist: (1) a fuller, more detailed account of her use of language; (2) an account of how the amoral egoist gives reasons for her actions both to herself and to others; and (3) an answer to the question in what sense her language and entire position is normative and in what sense it is not normative. These matters constitute an important segment of the argument in Chapters Six and Seven of Part III, where I push the amoral egoist on consistency questions, once I have exhibited amoral egoism as a viable alternative here in Part I.

7   This is a good spot to emphasize a limitation to my study. I do not attempt to provide an exhaustive account of the many different interpretations of "Why should I be moral?" that may be in use. I argue for the viability and philosophic interest of one very fundamental interpretation. For a discussion of some different ways that the question "Why should I be moral?" or the different question "Why should one be moral?" may be used, see chapter eleven of Bernard Gert's *Morality: A New Justification of the Moral Rules* (New York: Oxford University Press, 1989).

8   Plato, *Republic*, trans. G. M. A. Grube, revised by C. D. C. Reeve (Indianapolis: Hackett Publishing Company, Inc., 1992), p. 40 (365a-b).

9   Ibid., p. 29 (352d).

10 Plato, "Gorgias," in *The Collected Dialogues of Plato*, ed. Edith Hamilton and Huntington Cairns (New York: Bollingen Foundation, 1961), p. 270 (488a).

11 Plato, *Republic*, p. 40 (365b).

12 Plato, *The Republic of Plato*, trans. Francis M. Cornford (New York: Oxford University Press, 1945), p. 50.

13 To say that an individual has such an individual choice or decision to make does not preclude the possibility that the individual may reverse or redefine that fundamental decision. The revolution of fundamental concepts in the normative sphere is a fascinating topic, which cannot be pursued here.

14 Plato, *Republic*, trans. Grube-Reeve, pp. 289-90 (618b-e).

15 Compare Plato's approach with the position of Toulmin in the quote on page 9 above. In contrast to Toulmin, for Plato an important and difficult matter such as "the case for morality" needs to be confronted on philosophic grounds.

16 Taylor, *Principles of Ethics*, p. 225.

17 Ibid., pp. 226-27.

18 Plato, *Republic*, p. 41 (366c-d).

19 R. M. Hare, *Moral Thinking* (Oxford: Clarendon Press, 1981), see pp. 191-98.

20 Ibid., p. 198.

21 Plato, *Republic*, pp. 40-41 (365c).

22 Of course, within the *Republic,* Socrates does provide an answer to Glaucon's amoral challenge. I summarize the position. Socrates' answer is that the apparent profits an unjust man wins behind the veneer of the appearance of justice are illusory and insignificant compared with the self-inflicted harm his injustice brings upon the health of his own soul, "... a more valuable state than that of having a fine, strong, healthy body, since the soul itself is more valuable than the body ..." (Plato, *Republic,* p. 263 [591b]). Unlike the just man who has each of the parts of his soul in order with the godlike, philosophic part in control and enjoying the truest, purest, and most certain pleasures, the unjust man's pursuit of inferior and illusory pleasures results in the wild beast of his nature enslaving the godlike, philosophic part of one's soul. The question of whether the just life is better than the unjust life becomes under Socrates' account the question whether it is better to maintain or destroy the health of one's soul.

The key to evaluating Plato's argument rests with the alleged causal relationship between practicing injustice in the ethical sense and the consequential disorder of the soul (i.e., the Platonically defined psychological injustice as the improper functioning of the soul's parts). Plato's case is stronger in this area when pitted against Callicles' account of "natural justice" in the *Gorgias.* "... the naturally noble and just is what I now describe to you with all frankness—namely that anyone who is to live right should suffer his appetites to grow to the greatest extent and not check them, and through courage and intelligence should be competent to minister to them at their greatest and to satisfy every appetite with what it craves." (Plato, "Gorgias," in *Collected Dialogues,* p. 274 [491e-492a]). But the extreme case of the (psychologically) unjust within Socrates' account does not correspond to Glaucon and Adeimantus' original model of the unjust man. Socrates' unjust man is perfectly unjust in the psychological sense that his soul is in complete disorder with the philosophic part a slave to the passions. However, the perfectly unjust man in Glaucon's model is the artist who is discrete in his judgments, disciplined enough to maintain secrecy, and clever and controlled enough to "retrieve any mistake." Such an agent need not dissolve into a slave to the passions. In fact, the master of the craft of injustice may seek the "truest and most certain" pleasures by stealing the books of another or ruining a man's reputation in order to attain an academic post in which he can maximally enjoy the higher pleasures. Such a deceitful person may be the smoothest personality type in complete control, including having successfully deprogrammed her consciousness of the appropriateness of guilt feelings.

If one argues that Glaucon's artist of injustice cannot by definition have his Platonic self in order because, if he did, he would have wisdom which includes knowledge of the truth about justice, such an argumentative move begs the question as to which alternative life is the better life. Such a stipulation turns the Socratic argument against injustice into arguing that the unjust man's soul is extremely unhealthy because the unjust man is without justice. The Socratic tenet may be true that moral crime does not pay, given the metaphysical and psychological nature of human agency. But, as I understand it, Plato's account without supplementation does not successfully make the case. One gets the impression that Socrates' answer and Glaucon and Adeimantus' challenge do not squarely confront one another.

For further discussion of Socrates' answer, I recommend to the reader the following: Julia Annas, *An Introduction to Plato's Republic* (Oxford: Clarendon Press, 1981); Terence Irwin, *Plato's Moral Theory: The Early and Middle Dialogues* (Oxford: Clarendon Press, 1977); Richard Kraut, "The Defense of Justice in Plato's *Republic*" in Richard Kraut (ed.) *The Cambridge Companion to Plato* (New York: Cambridge University Press, 1992); C. D. C. Reeve, *Philosopher-Kings: The Argument of Plato's Republic* (Princeton: Princeton University Press, 1988); and Nicholas P. White, *A Companion to Plato's Republic* (Indianapolis, Hackett, 1979).

23 Immanuel Kant, *Critique of Practical Reason*, trans. Lewis White Beck (Indianapolis: Bobbs-Merrill, 1956), p. 36.

24 Immanuel Kant, *Religion Within the Limits of Reason Alone*, trans. Theodore M. Greene and Hoyt H. Hudson (New York: Harper & Row, 1960), p. 31.

25 Kant, *Critique*, p. 36.

26 Kant, *Religion*, pp. 31-32.

27 Hospers, *Human Conduct*, p. 194. For Hospers' complete discussion of "Why be Moral?" see the complete section, pp. 174-95.

28 Immanuel Kant, *Groundwork of the Metaphysic of Morals*, trans. H. J. Paton (New York: Harper & Row, 1964), pp. 109-10.

29 Kant, *Critique*, p. 37. Apparently Kant accounts for attempts to base morality on personal happiness in terms of theoretical antics which, like noise pollution, muffle the heavenly voice: "But (the practical conflict) can only maintain itself in the perplexing speculations of the schools which are audacious enough to close their ears to that heavenly voice in order to uphold a theory that costs no brainwork." Ibid., p. 36.

30 Joseph Butler,"Sermons and Dissertation Upon Virtue," in *British Moralists*, ed. L. A. Selby-Bigge (Indianapolis: Bobbs-Merrill, 1964), p. 230.

31 H. A. Prichard, "Duty and Interest" in *Readings in Ethical Theory*, ed. Wilfrid Sellars and John Hospers (New York: Appleton-Century-Crofts, 1952), p. 477.

32 Bradley,"Why Should I Be Moral?" p. 6.

33 Ibid., p. 3. Bradley here follows Kant's analogy of morality as personified: "... moral feeling still remains closer to morality and to its dignity in this respect: it does virtue the honour of ascribing to her *immediately* the approval and esteem in which she is held, and does not, as it were, tell her to her face that we are attached to her, not for her beauty but only for our own advantage." Kant, *Groundwork*, p. 110.

34 Henry Sidgwick, *The Methods of Ethics*, 7th ed. (Chicago: University of Chicago Press, 1907), p. 6.

35 Ibid., p. 14.

36 Ibid., p. 498.

37 Ibid., p. 508.

38 In his history of the development of his thought from the Preface to the 6th edition, Sidgwick notes that, "What [Aristotle] gave us [in his Ethics] was the Common Sense Morality of Greece, reduced to consistency by careful comparison: given not as something external to him but as what 'we'—he and others—think ascertained by reflection. Might I not imitate this: do the same for our morality here and now, in the same manner of impartial reflection on current opinion?" Ibid., pp. xix-xx.

39 In Chapters Six and Seven, with the advantage of a more in-depth discussion of the amoral egoist's reason-giving to himself and others, I will return to this discussion of the single method of the amoral egoist. At that point I will indicate in what sense the amoral egoist has a method, and the related question, whether such a method is a method of ethics in Sidgwick's sense.

40 Ibid., p. 13.

Part II

The Real Egoist

Chapter Three

The Real Egoist is a Personal Egoist

In the introductory chapter I indicated that a strongest-case analysis of the amoral egoist will involve teaming amoralism with a kind of egoism which is interesting, has empirical applicability and retains the spirit of egoism. I call this egoism *personal egoism*. The focus of this chapter is on distinguishing personal egoism from less challenging kinds.

What is special about personal egoism? A short answer to this question is simply "nothing"; it is not an unusual form of egoism, it is just a basic account of what a genuine egoist would be like. The real egoist is a personal egoist and the personal egoist is simply the real egoist.

The long answer to the question will run us through Chapter Seven, during which chapters I need to point out some "sporty features" of the basic egoistic model, which features become standard for those who are able to make use of them. However detailed my articulation of the position becomes in later chapters, my concern is to start with the original. If one is thoroughly egoistic, exclusively and fundamentally prescribing for one's own interests and advantage *regardless* of all other persons, then it is very important to ask questions such as: How would such a person conceptually organize her world of value, how does such an agent make plans that include other people, how does she strategize on a day-to-day basis, and what kinds of consistency are important for an egoist and why?

What some philosophers have done is what I call "ethicized" egoism, defined the position in such a way that it is a normative theory for everyone. As we shall see, in addition to other theoretical problems, the major problem with this approach to defining egoism is that no serious egoistic agent would ever hold it. Such theories have no empirical applicability. The egoist on the street would find these positions humorous, not attractive. To "ethicize" egoism is like putting an eagle into a small cage or, better yet, like freezing a snake—one has thereby lost touch altogether with how the creature moves, what it is, in the case of the egoist how she deceptively moves in a world peopled with many non-egoists. These egoism-for-everyone positions end up no longer talking about an agent who seriously prescribes a way of life for *herself alone* at the fundamental level.

Like Glaucon's perfectly unjust man, the amoral personal egoist who can pick her spots for immorality and under deceitful cover maintain the appearance of the moral person is no doubt the more challenging candidate. This kind of position can challenge morality in the very real sense of attracting our young people, and thereby corrupting the good will in our communities which is so very necessary for maintaining the basic moral practices and quality of personal relationships. The "ethicized" egoism-for-everyone candidates do not measure up to the real thing.

I begin my separation of personal egoism from other kinds by sketching the basic accounts of individual and universal egoism. I then will draw upon positions and arguments in key selected articles from the philosophic literature over the last thirty-some years in order to evaluate these two kinds of egoism in comparison with the basic personal egoist model. Appealing again to the model of the perfectly unjust man, individual, universal and personal egoism will each be evaluated in so far as each does or does not exhibit some articulated features of the perfectly unjust man. I will conclude the chapter with a brief discussion of the potential flexibility and rule-following practices of the personal egoist.

The discussion of egoism in contemporary philosophic literature has focused on two related issues: (1) whether egoism in one of its formulations qualifies as an ethical theory; and (2) whether egoism as an ethical theory is consistent. This latter issue becomes a two-part question: (a) is ethical egoism even initially consistent in its formulation;[1] and (b) even if initially consistent in formulation, is egoism *practically* inconsistent: that is, at the actual level of practice is it inconsistent for an ethical theorist to actually be an egoistic agent in application of her theory?

Answers to these two questions can vary widely depending upon which formulation of egoism one is focusing. For example, one type of egoism may be consistent in formulation and practice, but may not measure up to various qualifications which ethical theories are claimed to meet; on the other hand, a reformulated egoistic account may meet such qualifications but then fail to maintain consistency in some way.

In order to set out a working definition of the above-mentioned kinds of egoism, let each of the three be initially represented by a prescriptive statement indicative of its basic normative position:

a) *Universal* egoist: Everyone ought to seek her own self-interest and disregard the interests of all others in cases of conflict;

b) *Individual* egoist: Everyone ought to seek my (the individual egoist's) self-interest exclusively; and

c) *Personal* egoist: I (the personal egoist) ought to seek my own self-interest exclusively, the interests of others being valued only instrumentally as an aid in the pursuit of my singular goal.

Each of these egoistic forms will be clarified as needed in the context of this chapter's discussion.

CATEGORICAL EGOISM AT ISSUE, NOT HYPOTHETICAL EGOISM

At the start I point out an important distinction emphasized by Brian Medlin in his classic article "Ultimate Principles and Ethical Egoism." Medlin distinguishes between categorical and hypothetical egoism.

> The hypothetical egoist ... maintains that we all ought to observe our interest, because ... If we want such and such an end, we must do so and so (look after ourselves). The hypothetical egoist is not a real egoist at all.[2]

The hypothetical egoist may be a misguided utilitarian who holds that somehow the greatest sum total of happiness will be produced if every person goes for his own exclusively; or the hypothetical egoist could be one who strangely believes that God commands only egoistic motives for all human action. My concern here is with universal egoism, individual egoism, and personal egoism taken as categorical positions; that is, their egoistic positions are not held as a means to attaining some further end, but they are held simply because that is what we (or I) ought to do. Egoism as a fundamental principle is at issue.

Individual egoism

Individual egoism exhibits a problematic aspect of egoism as an ethical theory. William Frankena puts his finger on this problem area when he notes that the ethical egoist has two roles: one as an ethical *agent* who acts on her fundamental principle, and secondly, as a *spectator, adviser,* or *judge* in which role she says, *qua* theorist, what other agents should do, in the form of second- or even third-person judgments.[3] All the major problems of both the universal and individual forms of ethical egoism viewed as a theory of conduct stem from two basic questions: (1) whether the ethical egoist can successfully perform this "impersonal" advising or judging role, and (2) whether, in performing this advising role for others, the ethical egoist can remain a genuine, categorical egoist.

Frankena notes that ethical egoism when interpreted as individual egoism has a problem with the advising role:

> ... suppose that C and D are involved in some unpleasantness with one another and come to E for a judgment between them—a moral judgment, not a legal one. Then.(in so far as E is an individual egoist) E should base his judgment on a consideration, not of what is to C's or D's or the general advantage, but on what is to his own advantage. But surely we must regard such egoistically based advice and judgment as unsatisfactory and beside the point.[4]

Similarly, it is reasonable for an advocate of an ethical theory to tell others about it, to spread the word even if not explicitly asked for—in short, to give ethical advice. But, as Medlin argues, the individual egoist has a problem with this theoretical function:

> The (individual) egoist cannot promulgate that he is going to look after himself. He can't even preach that he *should* look after himself and preach this alone. When he tries to convince me that he should look after himself, he is attempting so to dispose me that I shall approve when he drinks my beer and steals Tom's wife. I cannot approve of his looking after himself and himself alone without so far approving of his achieving his happiness, regardless of the happiness of myself and others. So that when he sets out to persuade me that he should look after himself regardless of others, he must also set out to persuade me that I should look after him regardless of myself and others. Very small chance he has! And if the individual egoist cannot promulgate his doctrine without enlarging on it, what he has is no doctrine at all.[5]

Now the individual egoist who is not so comfortable with these theoretical and practical problems can go one of two ways. He can maintain his claim that he is advocating an ethical theory and slide over to universal egoism in an attempt to solve the above and other problems. Or, he can say to himself, "I don't need all these theoretical and practical problems of going public with my egoism. Forget that social sharing business. I'm going underground (as a personal egoist)." I turn first to the former option to see whether the universal version of ethical egoism can solve these problems.

UNIVERSAL EGOISM

Jesse Kalin, a contemporary defender of universal egoism, offers a decision procedure that includes the judging and advising functions of an ethical theory. The key to Kalin's formulation is a procedure for making normative judgments that jumps from favoring the interest of the judgment maker in the case of first-person judgments to focusing on the interest of the person talked to or talked about in the case of second- or third-person judgments. Kalin's universal egoism formulation consists of the following two principles:

(a) If A is judging about himself, then A is to use this criterion: A ought to do Y if and only if Y is in A's overall self-interest.

(b) If A is a spectator judging about anyone else, B, then A is to use this criterion: B ought to do Y if and only if Y is in B's overall self-interest.[6]

According to Kalin these conjoined principles provide consistent guidance because the first, second and third person judgments do not pull against one another for allegiance to the viewpoints of different agents. Distinguishing between yielding a contradiction and yielding a conflict, Kalin adds,

> Thus, the theory will have no difficulty in being an effective practical theory; it will not give contradictory advice, even in situations where interests conflict. True, it will not remove such conflicts—indeed it might well encourage them; but a conflict is not a contradiction.[7]

Of course, it is commonly thought that one of the key functions of an ethical theory is to resolve conflicts of interest. As John Hospers notes, in his important early article on egoism, impersonal or universal egoism does not provide a *rational* means of settling conflicts of interest, but it does provide a means, however less than ideal: it advises each party in a conflict to try to emerge victorious even though only one party can do so.[8] However, Hospers goes on to note a "curious tactical incongruity" in advising other people as such. Insofar as the universal egoist maintains (in some sense) an ethical theory, one would think that as a theorist the universal egoist would have an interest in the general acceptance of his theory. Yet, Hospers notes that tactics *qua* egoist may conflict with tactics *qua* theorist in the task of advising and promulgating:

> ... if I advise my business competitor to pursue his own interest with a vengeance, may he not follow my advice and pursue his interest so wholeheartedly that he forces me out of business? For the sake of my own interest, then, I may be well advised to keep my egoistic doctrine to myself, lest others use it against me.[9]

So we have with universal egoism a funny candidate for an ethical theory, such that the holder of such a theory must tactically remain silent about it and not share it with others, at least not in the interesting cases where it would make any practical difference. But this tactical problem of needing to severely limit or completely deny any exposure of one's theory, while at the same time claiming to have an ethical theory that can give guidance *for everyone*, is indicative of a problem deeper than that of when to talk about it.

Brian Medlin has a definite idea about where this deeper problem lies. He argues that if one holds universal egoism as a categorical position, and not merely a hypothetical one, the position is then at bottom based upon an inconsistent principle, inconsistent in the sense that the principle expresses two attitudes that are not compatible with one another: for example, "I want myself to come out on top and I don't care about Tom, ... " is not compatible with "I want Tom to come out on top and I don't care about myself ... . " Medlin goes on to say, although an inconsistent principle in the above sense, it is not contradictory. "This for the reason that we can, without contradiciton, express inconsistent desires and purposes ... . Don't we all want to eat our cake and have it too?" Although understandable in some sense, for Medlin such a principle can never be a successful first principle of ethics. "In so far as their desires conflict, people don't know what to do. And, therefore, no expression of incompatible desires can ever serve for an ultimate principle of human conduct."[10]

THE COMPETITIVE GAMES DEFENSE

The consistency of versions of universal egoism has been defended by focusing on the model of competitive games,[11] where a competitor may both want himself to win and want all others to *try* to win, emphasizing the universal guidance to *attempt* to attain what only one participant can achieve—success. John Hospers considers the possibility of an egoist who without qualification is willing to make his whole life into one single egoistic sport event by assembling Tom, Dick, Harry, etc. in one room and announcing publicly to all that "... each of you should try to come out on top."

> Perhaps the egoist likes to live life in a dangerous cut throat manner ... .
> He wants life to be spicy and dangerous; to him the whole world is one
> vast egoistic game, and living life accordingly is the way to make it
> interesting and exciting.[12]

Hospers' example of a possible egoist is instructive, but it fails to provide a successful defense of the consistency of universal egoism for two reasons. In the first place, such an egoist with a desire for the excitement that comes with maximal risk is a universal egoist only at the hypothetical level. Her hope for all others' trying to reach the top (even at her expense) is related in the following way to her own more basic personal egoism: If I want to have the greatest excitement in my egoistic life, then I ought to bring it about that all others seek their own interest also; hence, promulgation of a universal prescription such as "Everyone ought to seek her own self-interest ..." is the best way to fire up the competition. But note that such universal guidance of everyone is contingent upon her interest in the excitement of this sort of challenge. If the egoist's desires change, if she decides that she would rather live longer and pass over some possible excitement, then the universal guidance is no longer applicable.

THE PRIORITY PROBLEM OF THE EGOISTIC PLAYER-COACH

However, if we turn from the bold one-shot promulgation of egoistic thinking to consideration of a life of universal egoism over time, the basic difficulty with universal egoism as a practical program quickly surfaces. I call this basic difficulty of universal egoism the *priority problem of the player-coach*. Usually in the competitive arena of sports the organizer-coach is not a participant, but even if she is a player-coach who participates herself, never is one person the coach for *all* participants. A coach normally coaches one of two or more teams of participants. Using the athletic competitive model, the universal egoist is in the strange position of apparently coaching the competition to defeat herself *qua* participant, while at the same time *qua* participant doing everything she can to defeat the competition.

To add to Hospers' example, what does the universal egoist do if she finds out, after her initial bold promulgation of her organizing this egoistic game for all, that a good number of potential participants do not take her seriously? What if they band together in groups with "moralities" guiding their members? Should she gather them together again so that she can guide them toward getting it correct? But what if it is self-defeating or even disastrous to her participation to take the time or risk to organize and coach the other participants? At bottom, the problematic question for universal egoism is how can one really be an egoist and at the same time provide guidance for all others at the categorical level. In the sports analogy, it comes down to the question: is the universal egoist going to coach or play? One cannot *in practice* be a player-coach in the "game" called universal egoism.

Alan Gewirth in *Reason and Morality* capsulizes the practical problem of one who claims to be a universal egoist at the categorical level in terms of two dilemmas. In stating the first dilemma, Gewirth focuses on the universal egoist's nature of prescribing, when such an egoist claims that everyone ought to act for her own interest exclusively. In the case of the personal egoist, her endorsement and commitment to her own exclusive interest is unqualified and unambiguously clear. In the case of the universal egoist, when she categorically affirms that "everyone ought ...," her prescription or 'ought'-use either does or does not apply in the same way to all other persons. If the prescription for others has the same illocutionary use as prescriptions for herself only, such as "I ought ...," then the universal egoist is in effect endorsing the "oughts" of others in the very same way, in an unqualified and definitive way, as she endorses her own "oughts." Therefore, on this interpretation, the universal egoist is committed to incompatible, self-defeating directives.

On the other hand, if the universal egoist qualifies her prescriptions for others in a hypothetical way of the form: "If they are to play the game of life according to the rules of egoism, then they ought to act for their self-interest"; then the universal egoist's position is not truly universal for it does not apply in the same way to all persons. Gewirth summarizes,

> This, then is the universal ethical egoist's first dilemma. If he is to avoid upholding incompatible and self-defeating directives, he must at least incur equivocation, and his egoism cannot be universal. But if he avoids equivocation and maintains universality, he must uphold incompatible and self-defeating directives. [13]

Gewirth notes that the second dilemma arises once the universal egoist attempts to avoid such equivocation about her uses of "ought" by upholding that her unqualified and primary commitment is to the "Basic Rule of the Universal Egoistic Life-Game" in which each and every person ought to act for her own self-interest exclusively. But this primary endorsement in effect frustrates her achieving her own egoistic goals.

> Thus the egoist incurs a second dilemma. If he maintains his universal egoism with its primary, definitive commitment to the Formal Rules of the Universal Egoistic Life-Game, then he is not really an egoist in the sense of a person whose primary, definitive commitment is to the pursuit and maximization of his own self-interest, for he would endorse directives that violate his self-interest. If, on the other hand, he maintains this latter, egoistic commitment as his primary and definitive one, then he cannot maintain his *universal* egoism with its primary, definitive commitment to the universal life of struggle and conflict. [14]

One can try to avoid confronting this practical-inconsistency problem of trying to *be* a universal egoist by retreating to talk about the egoist's beliefs[15] that she entertains in a universal form. But as George Carlson has pointed out, it is one thing to believe universal egoism in some loose sense of *entertaining* egoism in a universal form; it is something else to *really believe* universal egoism in the stronger sense of not only entertaining the thought but also of "... being disposed to act in a way appropriate to (the egoist's) approving it as a principle of action for all ..."[16]

At bottom the tough question to answer is: how can one *be* a universal egoist, what does it mean to adopt as one's primary, unqualified normative commitment universal egoism? If the primary commitment is guiding all agents in the same way, then this egoistic stance with self-defeating, conflicting goals is a confused, atypical form of egoism. Or, if the primary normative commitment is to the agent's single goal of furthering her own self-interest exclusively, then, no matter what this egoistic agent *qua* theorist entertains as possible, her egoistic agency is not universal in the most important sense, but is clearly personal. To use our competitive game model, because of the nature of the egoistic "game," one cannot really be a player-coach that both participates egoistically and seriously coaches all other participants at the same time. Of course, one can be a player who entertains, at opportune moments, what she would say if she were a coach of her opponents in various situations. But that is another matter. In short, the charge of practical inconsistency is unavoidable for the universal egoist; she cannot at the categorical level successfully *be* what she claims to be.

EGOISTIC EFFICIENCY STANDARDS

In addition, from the sheer standpoint of efficiency, the universal and individual brands of egoism have built-in problems. George Carlson argues that to consider extending one's personal egoism to all others, by promulgating, advising, etc., is self-subverting and simply irrational in the sense of inefficacious, for such actions do not "... on the basis of the given information (which includes the good will of others) offer optimal prospects of achieving its (self-interested) objectives."[17] The simple support for his conclusion Carlson puts as follows:

> ... even if the egoist's advocacy of the individualistic axiom, as a comprehensive, overriding policy of action for all, fails to gain general acceptance (and the widespread injustice which would be detrimental with respect to his own interest, does not result), his own egoism will none the less be publicized in such a way as seriously to diminish the range of satisfactions available to him, because he will be prevented from surreptitiously taking advantage of the good will of others. In this way the universal egoist will be unable to combine regularly the advantages associated with his own injustices toward others and those associated with the justices of others toward him, and he will therefore fail to achieve the maximally advantageous amalgam, the realization of which was the *raison d'etre* for his egoism. [18]

To underline Carlson's point and also to relate the egoistic efficiency question to the question of what is the strongest egoistic challenge to morality, I turn to Glaucon and Adeimantus' account of the perfectly unjust man. How do universal egoism, individual egoism, and personal egoism each measure up to the four key features of the perfectly unjust man, which features explain in good part why the unjust life is so interesting a challenge to morality?

The first interesting feature of the life of the unjust man in Glaucon's account is that it is described and presented as a *genuine life-option* for an individual agent. Through his description of the interlocutors' actions, as well as by their words, Plato leaves no question that this life of injustice option does not just raise an academic question unrelated to everyday lives. At issue is the question of being one type of normative agent rather than another, thereby choosing a value framework in which to entrench oneself for the rest of one's life.

Against this criterion universal egoism fails miserably. A clear and consistent account of universal egoism as a primary practical option distinct from personal egoism has not been produced, while the defense of the position has drifted toward the position's alleged theoretical merits.[19]

The other three features of Glaucon's account of the unjust man are the following: (2) he takes careful account of the consequences of his actions, including maintaining the appearance of justice, thereby concealing "the greedy and crafty fox" of injustice behind a "... facade of illusory virtue";[20] (3) he is a consummate master of his craft; and (4) he is secretive to accomplish deceit. Glaucon includes these three features together in his description of the perfectly unjust man:

> First, therefore, we must suppose that an unjust person will act as clever craftsmen do: A first-rate captain or doctor, for example, knows the difference between what his craft can and can't do. He attempts the first but lets the second go by, and if he happens to slip, he can put things right. In the same way, an unjust person's successful attempts at injustice must remain undetected, if he is to be fully unjust. Anyone who is caught should be thought inept, for the extreme of injustice is to be believed to be just without being just. And our completely unjust person must be given complete injustice; nothing may be subtracted from it. We must allow that, while doing the greatest injustice, he has nonetheless provided himself with the greatest reputation for justice. If he happens to make a slip, he must be able to put it right. If any of his unjust activities should be discovered, he must be able to speak persuasively or to use force. And if force is needed, he must have the help of courage and strength and of the substantial wealth and friends with which he has provided himself.[21]

On these three criteria, both the individual and universal egoist, far from being masters of their craft of egoism, simply display themselves as bunglers. By openly participating *qua* egoists in morality-type activities, such as advising, promulgating, and defending their egoism, the individual and universal egoists exhibit a self-defeating disregard for their appearances of attitude and character and a disregard for any careful account of the consequences of their advising and theorizing.

Therefore, only the personal egoist has any chance of measuring up to the standard of Glaucon and Adeimantus' unjust man; only the personal egoist can present a genuine practical option while keeping her position a secret to all, maintaining her appearances and handling her actions' consequences as a master of her craft. For these reasons I make the very easy choice of teaming personal egoism with amoralism as the only egoism that makes sense as a distinctive normative option. My clarified version of "Why should I be moral?" can now be understood as the question, "Why should I be moral rather than being an amoral personal egoist?"

NECESSARY SKILLS IN THE CRAFT OF EGOISM

I turn now to an initial brief discussion of some of the skills of thought and language that the amoral personal egoist must have if she is to be successful in her craft. To introduce this discussion, I confront an objection to my whole attempt, both here and throughout the following five chapters, to describe an interesting and challenging amoral personal egoist.

The objection is that, if the personal egoist can ony escape inconsistency by being a mindless brute, who cares?! A mindless brute as a practical alternative may be a genuine alternative, but as such is certainly not interesting. Bernard Williams put it this way:

> We shall reasonably be unimpressed by the egoist if the territory which he can consistently and rationally occupy is too constricted. Of course a man can be consistent by having no, or very few, thoughts; and that some dismal self-seeking brute can satisfy the egoist specification I shall take to be of little interest. The egoist will be more interesting vis-a-vis morality if as well as having a fair range of territory to operate in, he should be moreover moderately attractive, where that means moderately attractive to us.[22]

The full range and boundaries of the personal egoist's territory of operations I will continue describing in subsequent chapters, culminating in Chapter Eight with a discussion of important limitations to being an amoral personal egoist. My purpose here is simply to suggest that the personal egoist need not be a mindless brute, that she may, in fact, display considerable conceptual and linguistic sophistication in following rules and in socializing with other human agents.

The amoral personal egoist holds, as her fundamental procedural principle and orientation to all of life's transactions with other persons, that she ought to pursue her own wants exclusively and disregard the wants of all others, unless the satisfaction of the want of another person is at the same time recognized as a means to satisfy a priority want of the egoist. Accordingly, all personal goals and forward-looking decisions are evaluated, and all past egoistic judgments are judged as correct or foolish, in light of the fundamental egoistic principle—the key to all internal justification.

Although, as an amoralist, the amoral personal egoist will have no primary concern in guiding her actions according to a set of interpersonally respected moral rules, she will find it useful to *make rules for herself*. The need for rules arises in classifying possible alternative actions and in prescribing how the egoist should treat others in different kinds of describable situations. One way that the egoist may use practical rules is in situations where the probabilities of consequential outcomes are somewhat unclear; in these cases the egoist may use prudential rules as "rules of thumb" or handy "sign posts" in calculating her best outcome. Also in recurring situations which are not opportune for a big payoff, egoistic calculation is difficult to maintain at a high peak of alertness and concentration. In these situations, the risks of self-defeating inefficiencies, due to inadvertant lapses in concentration, may be sufficiently great to rely as far as possible on a prepared set of prudential "rules of thumb."

In discussing utilitarian calculation, J. J. C. Smart, following Sidgwick, notes that in certain kinds of decision-making situations the correct extreme or act utilitarian conclusion is most often arrived at, not by thinking *qua* extreme utilitarian, but by trusting to common sense morality.[23] One such case, Smart discusses, is the case in which one's calculations may tend to be biased in one's own favor, in situations of deep personal involvement. For example, in deciding to divorce one's spouse, one may exaggerate one's own unhappiness and underestimate the resulting harm to the children of a broken home. However, for the egoist there is nothing problematic about being partial to one's own interests as such—it is the whole ball game; but the egoist's being biased toward a single, individual want may be analogously problematic. In situations conducive to the satisfaction of a single want, the egoist must be careful not to ruin satisfaction opportunities for many other, possibly higher order, wants. Like Smart's worry about the accuracy of utilitarian calculation in situations of deep personal involvement, so too the egoist will be concerned to avoid miscalculating the overall disastrous consequences of indulging a single anarchistic want in enticing circumstances. Prudence may prescribe rigorous rule-following to avoid Platonic intemperance in the egoistic soul that is intent on eliminating all inefficiency in the carefully ordered satisfaction of all its primary wants.

In addition to evaluating consequences with respect to a carefully designed hierarchy of potentially conflicting wants, the calculations of the clever and disciplined egoist will include intricate estimations of both short- and long-term consequences. For example, the egoist experienced in business may use it as a "rule of thumb" not to cheat her clients in situations of class X because she wants their business five years down the road.

The most distinctive characteristic of the egoist's calculations, which radically differentiates it from all other deliberation procedures, is the *maintenance of secrecy* about her egoism and about her total absence of genuine good will. It is very inefficient to *appear* to be completely biased in her own favor. Especially in everyday affairs, which are highly repetitive and consistently cluttered with the same group of human resources and obstacles, one of the most efficacious tactics possible is to avoid being categorized as having a selfish character, much less being a card-carrying egoist. The clever egoist realizes that inefficient strategies or tactical moves at inopportune moments may be self-defeating and needlessly tip her hand.

It is this risk of detection and its efficiency costs that are crucial in explaining the egoist's second kind of rule-following, which comes to play in situations in which the detection risk is so great that normal egoistic calculation is itself inefficient and must be temporarily suspended. At his leisure in a "cool hour," the clever egoist will design a set of rules to be strictly adhered to in these special circumstances, along with corresponding sets of criteria for the easy recognition of those situations with sufficient detection risk to warrant a black-out on egoistic calculation. When planning some specific strategy in a "cool hour" or when calculating on the "battle field" but not in a danger area, the clever egoist will make use of prudential rules as "rules of thumb," as handy "sign posts" to direct his way; but, once the egoist reads a situation to be a detection danger area of kind X, then he will follow religiously an appropriate set of prescriptions, the adherence to which *constitutes* his carefully designed and far-sighted *practice* of maximizing efficiency in the satisfaction of ordered wants A, B, C, ... , in situations of class X. It is in this context of maintaining normative secrecy via practice-defining rule-following that it does make sense to say that a genuine egoist may be a rule egoist.

In summary, while having no respect for interpersonal moral rules as such, the amoral personal egoist will adopt and make use of his own egoistic rules in order to be maximally efficient *qua* egoist in his interactions with others. In adopting complex sets of both rules of thumb and constitutive rules, the amoral personal egoist thereby can set up a sophisticated internal justification system requiring careful and conscientious application. Far from a mindless brute having few thoughts, such rule making and rule application requires considerable sophistication in thought and in articulation.

Notes

1 A classical attempt to refute ethical egoism as inconsistent in its very formulation is the argument of G. E. Moore in *Principia Ethica* (Cambridge: Cambridge University Press, 1903; paperback reprint ed. 1966). Moore defines ethical egoism as, "... each man ought rationally to hold: My own greatest happiness is the only good thing there is..." (p. 97). Moore argues, "The only reason I can have for aiming at 'my own good' is that it is *good absolutely* ... . But if it is *good absolutely* that I should have it, then everyone else has as much reason for aiming at *my* having it, as I have myself ... . What Egoism holds, therefore, is that *each* man's happiness is the sole good – that a number of different things are *each* of them the only good thing there is--an absolute contradiction! No more complete and thorough refutation of any theory could be desired" (p. 99).

In his essay "Certain Features in Moore's Ethical Doctrines," appearing in editor P. A. Schilpp's *The Philosophy of G. E. Moore*, 2d ed. (New York: Tudor Publishing Co., 1952), C. D. Broad's defense of ethical egoism centers on Moore's formulation of the thesis. Broad argues that the ethical egoist "... will assert that it is not his duty to produce good experiences and dispositions as such, without regard to the question of who will have them"

(p. 45). Broad goes on to point out that what ethical egoism does contradict is, not itself but, Sidgwick's second axiom about goodness and our obligations to produce it. "This is stated as follows in Book III, Chapter XII of Sidgwick's *Methods of Ethics* (382, in 6th ed.): – '... as a rational being I am bound to aim at good generally – so far as it is attainable by my efforts – not merely at a particular part of it' " (p. 45). See also Moore's reply to Broad in the same volume.

This interchange by Moore and Broad points out what I will emphasize in this chapter, that how egoism is formulated or described is the key to its success or failure on grounds of either theoretical or practical consistency.

2　Brian Medlin,"Ultimate Principles and Ethical Egoism," *Australasian Journal of Philosophy* 35 (1957): 111-18, reprinted in David P. Gauthier, ed., *Morality and Rational Self-Interest* (Englewood Cliffs, N.J.: Prentice-Hall, 1970), p. 59.

3　Frankena, *Ethics*, pp. 16-17.

4　Ibid., pp. 17-18.

5　Medlin, "Ultimate Principles," p. 58.

6　Jesse Kalin,"In Defense of Egoism" in Gauthier, *Morality and Rational Self-Interest*, pp. 67-69.

7　Ibid., p. 70.

8　John Hospers, "Baier and Medlin on Ethical Egoism," *Philosophical Studies* 12 (1961): 13.

9　Ibid.

10　Medlin,"Ultimate Principles," p. 63.

11　See, for example, Jesse Kalin, in "On Ethical Egoism," *American Philosophical Quarterly*, Monograph Series No. 1 (1968), pp. 33-35, and in "Two Kinds of Moral Reasoning: Ethical Egoism as a Moral Theory," *Canadian Journal of Philosophy* 5 (1975): 324-34, esp.

12　Hospers, "Baier and Medlin," p. 16.

13　Alan Gewirth, *Reason and Morality* (Chicago: University of Chicago Press, 1978), p. 85.

14　Ibid., p. 87.

15　See Kalin's reply to Gewirth's critique of universal egoism in Kalin's "Public Pursuit and Private Escape: The Persistence of Egoism" in Edward Regis Jr., ed., *Gewirth's Ethical Rationalism* (Chicago: University of Chicago Press,

1984), pp. 128-46. See also Gewirth's reply in turn to Kalin in his "Replies to My Critics," pp. 215-19, in the same volume.

[16] George R. Carlson, "Ethical Egoism Reconsidered," *American Philosophical Quarterly* 10 (1973): p. 29.

[17] Ibid., p. 26.

[18] Ibid.

[19] See Kalin, "Two Kinds of Moral Reasoning," p. 355, where Kalin talks of the "egoist as an ethical theorist" who may be motivated by his disenchantment with some version of morality and may be interested in a theoretical replacement.

[20] Plato, *Republic*, p. 40 (365c).

[21] Ibid., p. 36 (360e-361b).

[22] Bernard Williams, *Problems of the Self* (Cambridge: Cambridge University Press, 1973), p. 251.

[23] J. J. C. Smart, "Extreme and Restricted Utilitarianism," in Michael F. Wagner, ed., *An Historical Introduction to Moral Philosophy* (Englewood Cliffs, N.J.: Prentice Hall, 1991), p. 217.

Chapter Four

Morality or Simply Egoistic Strategy?

In Chapter Two I argued that the key to the viability of and interest in my interpretation of the question "Why should I be moral?" lies in the genuine fundamental alternative itself, being moral or being an amoral egoist. In Chapter Three I argued for the specification of personal egoism as the only form of egoism that measures up to the question's amoral challenge. In making this comparative evaluation of personal egoism, as against universal and individual egoism, the amoral egoistic option was thereby examined and further clarified. In Chapter Four my focus turns to the other fundamental normative option, being moral.

More specifically, I examine some key contemporary accounts of being moral and appraise whether or not these accounts have the capacity to provide a genuine normative alternative to the life of an amoral personal egoist. I show that procedural and definitional choices in these accounts of being moral fail to provide a distinct option which is not conceptually swallowed up by the concept of a sophisticated amoral personal egoist. By exhibiting these unsuccessful theoretical choices, I will emphasize by contrast those key conceptual and procedural elements of my argument that are essential to developing the integral challenge of the question "Why should I be moral rather than an amoral personal egoist?"

At issue here is not only that some accounts of morality slide into egoistic accounts but more importantly *why* these accounts can be redescribed as simply optional egoistic strategies. Like Glaucon and Adeimantus' challenge that some reasons for being just can also justify a deceptive life of injustice provided the appearances are handled well, I argue that these contemporary accounts of morality can just as well be explained as simply strategy options within a purely egoistic game plan.

In the chapter's first part, I show that an account of being moral behavioristically defined in terms of conformity to social rules is perfectly consistent with being an amoral personal egoist, that on this account the question of being moral becomes just a matter of opting for a certain set of conservative egoistic tactics. I argue (a) that within such an account the amoral challenge loses interest because the crucial distinction between being moral and seeming to be moral loses its point, and (b) that, in spite of the limitations of such a behavioristic account, the genuine and interesting question remains: Why should I be moral rather than an amoral personal egoist?

I then look at two very important contemporary accounts of "Why should I be moral?" by Kurt Baier and Kai Nielsen. I argue that neither account pushes the question far enough. However, the limitations of each account, including the common failure to sufficiently articulate the distinct normative alternatives of being moral and being egoistic, help indicate the way toward the most promising solution. In the case of Kurt Baier, I will show that Baier severely handicaps his account at the very start by embracing the assumption he shares with Hobbes, that first-person reasons are always self-interested reasons. As a result, Baier's good-reasons argument is asked to do more than it can do. The good-reasons argument with its two limited theoretical scenarios, everyone suffering the consequences of the Hobbesian "state of Nature" or everyone acting from a "God's-eye point of view," just does not have the theoretical equipment to handle the challenge of the amoral egoist, the free rider who prefers to retain an exclusively first-person and self-interested point of view.

In the more promising account of Kai Nielsen, the question "Why should I be moral?" is analyzed in terms of a fundamental choice between two alternative points of view. His argument at bottom is that, given human beings with their needs and wants as we know them, there are strong self-interested reasons for an individual person "not to override moral considerations" and "become a moral agent" with a moral point of view. In evaluating Nielsen's argument, I argue that there no doubt is a sense in which an individual can "become a moral agent" for purely self-interested reasons, but in this sense the argument then simply amounts to showing that an amoral egoist has good self-interested reasons to *appear* to be of good morals by tactically showing "good morals" activity most of the time. The limitations of Nielsen's definition of the egoist as exhibiting a "persistent policy of selfishness" are contrasted with features of the concept of an egoist who is selectively immoral but takes full account of all consequences as a master of her craft.

In the chapter's third part, I turn to the unique account of morality by Jesse Kalin. In Kalin's case, the fundamental normative alternatives are not distinctly articulated simply because he attempts to eliminate completely the alternative to egoism, by attempting to theoretically reduce morality to a special form of egoism. I show that Kalin's reduction attempt is not only exceedingly far from the mark in attempting to descriptively capture what morality is, but Kalin's theoretical maneuverings result in drastic changes in language use and reasoning, including embracing a relativism that can be turned on Kalin himself, when he attempts to defend his egoism and reduce morality to it. A by-product of my analysis of Kalin will be the further clarification of the amoral personal egoist whose agency stands in sharp contrast to the confusing picture of the agent attempting to compete in Kalin's universal game of life.

MORALITY AS BEHAVIOR CONFORMITY

According to T. L. S. Sprigge, a moral code is very much like a society's unwritten legal code, a system of rules promulgated and encouraged by public opinion. The violation of this unwritten code is punished informally by the withdrawal of affection and friendliness, along with the refusal of services. Sprigge explains individual conscience in terms of the internalization of the operation of the moral sanction. Conscience serves as an internal representative of society, the punisher of nonconformity, once the individual "... has learnt to dislike himself for acting in certain ways by being made to feel disliked by others for acting in cetain ways."[1] Being moral on Sprigge's account then consists in conforming one's conduct to such a socially sanctioned code.

In Sprigge's behavioristic account of morality two questions come to the fore: On the one hand, what does the question, "Why should I be moral?" amount to asking and, secondly, does Sprigge's account provide a distinct normative option to that of being an amoral personal egoist?

Regarding the former question, given this quasi-legal notion of morality, the unanalyzed "Why should I be moral?" becomes a question such as, why is it in my best interest to conform to society's code of conduct, given the external and internal sanctions against infringement? Note the similarity to the question, why is it in my self-interest to be law-abiding or will crime pay for me? The most naive criminal soon discovers that, in infringing most of the laws most of the time, the price of non-conformity is clearly rather extravagant. Similarly, taken as an over-the-long-haul question as to what is generally in one's self-interest, no doubt about it, moral conformity also pays. However, whether it pays for a particular individual to be a qualified moral conformist, who may deviate from some of society's codes in special opportunistic circumstances, may involve very complex calculation. But, no matter how complex, the procedure of deliberation is always: are the advantages of non-conformity worth the price paid in the coin of moral sanctions, given their probability of occurrence, their degree, their extent, etc.? For example, honesty is no doubt the best policy for Kant's small-town grocer[2] in handling the children's pennies, but it may not be for Slick Sam who finds a naive traveling salesman suddenly in need of a used car with which to finish his monthly rounds.

Turning to the second question, does Sprigge's account of morality provide a genuine alternative to being an amoral personal egoist? I argue that it does *not* provide such a genuine option. "Why should I be moral?" on this account of being moral is a question about personal efficiency and damage control, which is quite compatible with the strategy of the amoral personal egoist. In fact, does not the following egoistic question of tactics parallel the question "Why should I be moral?" when the latter is interpreted in this way:

> Why, as an egoist, is it the most efficient policy in seeking maximal want satisfaction to choose as my primary practical guidelines that set of rules which are at the same time the widely recognized prohibitions of conventional morality?

For the proper characterization of the practical agent who raises *exclusively* self-interested questions from the first-person singular frame of reference is an egoist; and the egoist's judgments of conformity and non-conformity simply become a matter of everyday calculation of consequential pay-offs.

Note that this strategy question from the trench of personal egoism is a very different question than the more basic question about why should I entrench myself in one or the other of these fundamental normative options *in the first place*. While Plato recognized the interesting strategic questions about "saving the appearances" of justice from the point of view of the unjust man, his primary concern was with the more basic question about philosophically defending the choice between entrenching oneself in one or the other of two distinct kinds of normative agency. Similarly, my focus is on a question about two distinct kinds of normative agency, being moral or being an amoral personal egoist, rather than on a less fundamental question about practical strategies from within one or the other of the two life-defining agencies.

Furthermore, in addition to failing to provide for a genuine normative option to being an amoral personal egoist, it is important to note that Sprigge's social conformity account does not silence nor render unimportant my question about the character of agency. For underlying all practical questions about strategy within a given type of normative agency, whether to be risky, conforming, dramatic or whatever, lies the question about accepting or maintaining that normative agency itself. This latter question of agent morality drives to the heart of ethics and normative acceptability.

Notice too that my observations about this social conformity account of morality are not affected if one complicates Sprigge's simple notion of morality. One can assume that the ethical agent's "conscience" is not a mere internalized representative of an external social sanction process, and that one can prescribe for oneself sophisticated guidelines given the priority of one's most basic wants, in light of a careful estimate of one's interest-pushing abilities and of the availability of one's resources, and with due consideration to legal punishments and the informal sanctions of public opinion. Nevertheless, as long as "being moral" is defined behavioristically as mere conformity to societal rules and as long as first-person reasons are assumed to be exclusively a matter of self-interested efficiency, the question of opting for morality or not loses substance. Gone is any genuine opposition between being moral and being amoral and egoistic; gone are the opposing epithets of "utterly naive" and "utterly contemptible"; we are left only with the more or less clever. But to get beyond the discussion of mere strategic efficiency is to ask for the evaluation of that efficiency in light of some more basic criteria. One fundamental practically important question about basic evaluatory criteria is the question: "Why should I be moral rather than an amoral personal egoist?"

MORAL REASONS AS SUPERIOR REASONS

In his classic book, *The Moral Point of View*, Kurt Baier begins a key part of his argument in chapter two, where he argues that the general question "What shall I do?" "... comes to much the same as 'What is *the best* thing I can do?"[3] In considering criteria for evaluating what is the best thing to do, Baier notes that a human action is not only judged the best choice by reason of its efficiency in bringing about an agent's purpose, but it also may be evaluated in light of the agent's purpose itself.

> ... we can always ask whether what the agent is aiming at is the best thing to aim at. Frequently, when someone asks, "What shall I do?" he is not merely asking which is the better course of action, *given a certain aim or end*, but which of several ends or aims is the best.[4]

Baier then goes on to state that the best course of action is "... *the course of action which is supported by the best reasons.*"[5]

In chapter seven entitled "Why Should We Be Moral?" Baier argues that the best reasons are moral reasons, superior to all other reasons, including self-interested reasons.

> The very *raison d'etre* of a morality is to yield reasons which overrule the reasons of self-interest in those cases when everyone's following self-interest would be harmful to everyone. Hence moral reasons are superior to all others.[6]

Baier goes on to explain that he means, not only that we do in fact so regard moral reasons, but also that we ought to so regard them as superior. A key to his argument is the following comparison of hypothetical worlds.

> The answer is that we are now looking at the world from the point of *anyone*. We are not examining particular alternative courses of action before this or that person; we are examining two alternative worlds, one in which the reverse is the practice. And we can see that the first world is the better world, because we can see that the second world would be the sort which Hobbes describes as the state of nature.This shows that I ought to be moral, for when I ask the question "What ought I to do?" I am asking, "Which is the course of action supported

by the best reasons?" But since it has just been shown that moral reasons are superior to reasons of self-interest, I have been given a reason for being moral, for following moral reasons rather than any other, namely, they are better reasons than any other.[7]

Baier's argument is largely convincing when viewed as merely an answer to the first-person plural question, "why should *we* be moral?" It is better for everyone that society's members function with an ongoing system of guidance and social control, rather than with absolutely none at all. The alternative, so graphically described by Hobbes, is disastrous for everyone. But Baier's argument is less convincing as an answer to the first-person singular question, for the argument is the same for both questions: Acting on moral reasons is acting on superior reasons because one possible world A is a better hypothetical world than world B. However, in the case of the first-person singular question, the argument is asked to carry too much. In the first place, why is one limited to just these two hypothetical worlds? For instance, why could not a single person follow moral rules most of the time, and thereby act on the "best reasons" as defined by the two-worlds conception; and yet for the rest of the time, why not override those superior moral reasons and act on self-interested reasons, especially if one's bad example, if detected, is not detrimental to the future healthy functioning of society's moral system?

Another way of critically questioning Baier's two-worlds argument from the first-person singular point of view is the following: in evaluating the normative practices in alternative worlds, why cannot agent A focus on that possible world in which everyone else acts on moral reasons except agent A; whereas agent A overrides moral reasons and acts for her own self-interest each and every time she can do so successfully with respect to her long-range best interest. In this case why cannot agent A define such a world as the best possible world (for A, of course)? If so, then A could also be said to always act for the best reason (for A).

One might say in defense of Baier's account that he is "... looking at the world from the point of view of *anyone*," that he is considering only reasons that are equally applicable to all persons in society. The problem with this reply is that there is no further reasoning in Baier's account to warrant his partiality to "the point of view of anyone" and his exclusion of agent A's arbitrary "superior reasons" (for A). His comparison of the two (only) worlds is important to making the case for our having a moral system in society, but this limited hypothetical argument is no help in defending his applying his superior reasons argument to the first-person singular point of view.[8]

Of course, one response to agent A's free riding and attachment only to his self-interested "best world" is that such activity and normative planning is just not fair! But then the question "Why should I be fair?" is a relevant question, as is "Why should I be unfair?" Of course, the more interesting question is again the more fundamental question: not "Why should I be fair or unfair in this particular situation?" but rather "Why should I be a fair person rather than a person who may be unfair in each and every case in which unfairness pays?" This latter question is about being one kind of normative agent rather than another, a version of "Why should I be moral rather than an amoral personal egoist?"

The challenge of the amoral personal egoist is just this sort of challenge at the fundamental level of agency. The agent who questions and rejects all distinctively moral points of view is an agent who has no interest in the "point of view of anyone." Similarly, as I will discuss in considerable detail in Chapter Seven, in rejecting the moral way of life the amoral personal egoist also rejects the special reasoning of morality including reasoning from the point of view of anyone: only the egoistic imperative and its applications are practically germane to what such an agent judges she ought to do. Everything else is "egoistically inferior."

To answer the question, why does Baier need his superior reasons-hypothetical worlds argument to accomplish more than it can accomplish, involves focusing on that key Baier assumption that he shares with Thomas Hobbes: the only reasons for action are self-interested reasons. But from exclusively self-interested reasons one can only get to the moral construct of "the point of view of everyone" by focusing on a hypothetical world in which such a point of view pays for every agent. But at the very start did not Baier give Hobbes too much? Relevant is the question, why should I reason exclusively from a self-interested point of view in the first place? It is because of this assumption about exclusively self-interested reasons that Baier can only construct a common point of view by bringing in talk of a hypothetically best world, unfortunately without any theoretic justification from within his account.

LIMITED PATTERNS OF IMMORALITY

I turn now to the account of "Why should I be moral?" by Kai Nielsen. As noted in the introductory chapter, Kai Nielsen has defended the question "Why should I be moral?" against many-sided criticism as a legitimate question, neither meaningless nor pointless. In one of these criticisms John Hospers raised the objection that the question is a self-contradictory request.[9] Nielsen begins his reply to Hospers by agreeing that the question is indeed contradictory, but only if it is asked as a self-interested question. He then adds,

> But is there any reason for me always to act from one point of view rather than another when I am a member in good standing in a moral community? True enough, Hospers has shown me that from the moral point of view I have no alternative but to try to do what is right and from a self-interested point of view I have no rational alternative but to act according to what I judge to be in my rational self-interest. But what I want to know is what I am to do: Why adopt one point of view rather than another? Is there a good reason for me, placed as I am, to adopt the moral point of view or do I just arbitrarily choose, as the subjectivist would argue?[10]

Nielsen goes on to say that, when the issue is understood at its fundamental level, there is no philosophically definitive alternative to subjectivism, no practical alternative to the existentialists' plight. One must just ultimately decide what kind of person to be, without the aid of an ultimately valid criterion of rationality. The moral and self-interested points of view, Nielsen argues, each have their own separate spheres in practical discourse with distinct canons of rationality and justificatory criteria.

> There can be no complete non-personal, objective justification for acting morally rather than non-morally. . . . We have two policies of action to choose from, with distinct criteria of appropriateness and which policy of action will make us happy will depend on the sort of person we *happen* to be.[11]

Nielsen's subjectivism at the fundamental level and its relevance to answering "Why should I be moral rather than an amoral personal egoist" I save for discussion in my final chapter. Some key questions to be raised there will be: How does Nielsen know when all the philosophic work is done and how are such existential choices and the reasons for these choices connected?

In spite of his metaethical subjectivism, Nielson does go on to argue that there are two related generalizations that can be made with confidence about the relation between a self-interestedly pursued life of immorality and personal happiness: (a) to live a life style that is thoroughly and completely selfish or immoral will produce miserable results for oneself, as well as for others; and (b) there are good self-interested reasons for a person to *generally* act in accordance with society's moral practices. How Nielsen discusses these limited claims will exhibit also the limitations of his two key concepts under scrutiny, being an amoral egoist and being moral, and thereby will provide some direction toward the kind of analyses of the respective moral and egoistic agencies that are needed.

Nielsen argues that in cases involving ". . . certain specific acts that go against the requirements of morality . . ." [or]

> . . . for *limited patterns of behavior*, no decisively good reasons can be given to some individuals that would justify their doing the moral thing in such a context. (It would be another thing again if they repeatedly acted in that way. Here the case for morality would be much stronger).[12]

In *Reason and Practice* Nielsen writes:

> Occasional immoral acts are quite compatible with a happy life for the immoralist, but a thorough and consistent pattern of wrongdoing will, as the world goes, make for him and for those about him a little circle of misery. . . . Viewed purely in the abstract, there indeed is and can be no question-begging answer to the question "Why should I be moral?" However, for human beings as we find them . . . consistently failing to act in accordance with a moral point of view will lead to a miserable life for the person who so acts. In short, there are solid self-interested reasons for a man not to override moral considerations. Indeed, only to be a man of good morals is not, as Kant stressed, to be a morally good man, but there are generally good self-interested reasons for becoming genuinely unselfish and for becoming a moral agent. We have good reasons, as individuals . . . , not only to support that system of social control . . . , but also generally to act in accordance with a moral system of social control ourselves.[13]

BECOMING A PERSON OF GOOD MORALS

In evaluating Nielsen's arguments, several definitional points need to be made at the start for reasons of clarity. First of all, it is clear that Nielsen's primary use of "being moral" is in a behavioristic, conforming sense, as acting "... in accordance with a moral system of social control." Nielsen does note that "... only to be a man of good morals is not, as Kant stressed, to be a morally good man, but there are generally good self-interested reasons for becoming genuinely unselfish and for becoming a moral agent." However, apparently Nielsen is only indicating to the reader that he is aware that this distinction can be made and proceeds to use only the one sense of being moral, as being a man of good morals in the behavioristic-conforming sense. He does not pursue the delineation of what it would be to be a morally good man, nor does he explain how "genuinely unselfish" differs from being a man of good morals with a (more) limited pattern of selfish behavior, nor what is involved in becoming a moral agent for self-interested reasons? Careful answers to these important questions could have provided Nielsen with the tools to expand his argument beyond its definitional limitations.

A second definitional point involves Nielsen's apparent confusing the *continually* immoral person with the amoral person. Regarding the amoral point of view, Nielsen states,

> It is evident that by so acting he is being immoral, since he is persistently and self-consciously free-loading by accepting the benefits of a society organized on a moral basis without accepting any of its responsibilities or liabilities. ... . He takes advantage of the goodwill and commitment to morality of others without exhibiting goodwill himself or taking any of the risks or sharing the burdens essential to the continued existence of the system of social control that is admittedly beneficial to all. This kind of unfairness is the quintessence of immorality.[14]

I agree completely with Nielsen that the free-loading amoralist is and ought to be roundly judged to be immoral, in the sense that such an attitude or viewpoint is itself immoral insofar as it is disposed to pursue occurrent immoral acts, whether of the unfair, dishonest, or harmful variety, all the while enjoying the advantages of morality's social order and stability. However, the clever amoral egoist need not engage in occurrent, individual immoral acts all the time, or even much of the time. The informed and disciplined amoral egoist will engage in actions transgressing prevailing moral practices only when so doing will involve relatively little or no risk of negative social consequences and when the egoistic calculation of personal gain per effort is very positive. This sort of amoral egoist, of course, knows that a "thorough and consistent pattern of wrongdoing" will make for herself and others around her "a little circle of misery." As discussed in Chapter Three, such crude, unenlightened egoism never pays.

However, this is altogether different from a thorough and consistent pattern of acting on amorally egoistic grounds as such. Such amorally egoistic grounds, in fact, prescribe both constitutive rules and general cautionary guideposts which respectively rule out and warn against immorality in situations x, y, and z for reasons of egoistic efficiency. Similarly, an amoral egoist, who guides her own actions consistently with her own self-interest solely in mind, need not be crudely selfish in her carefully chosen actions; for such behavior would be self-defeating. In discussing the disadvantages of egoism spreading in society, Nielsen writes:

> And, if too many go the way of the rational individual egoist, then it will no longer pay to be non-moral so that large numbers of individual egoists, if they are rational, will become men of good morals.[15]

Here again, Nielsen's definitional choices are misleading. When the societal situation becomes more challenging, the amoral egoist does not have to become anything other than what she is—an amoral egoist. For tactical reasons she may judge it most efficient in these circumstances to temporarily expand her conforming behavior and take greater care about the success and example of her immoral deeds, in order to maintain the *appearance* of a person of good morals. But in all situations the amoral egoist will be immoral only for, in Nielsen's words, "limited patterns of behavior," namely when those patterns are promising of a clear payoff. So the enlightened amoral egoist, if she is clever, can combine in a single, consistently applied way *both* limited patterns of immorality with a general conformity to society's prevailing moral system of control—again because the combination is egoistically efficient.

An amoralist who is selective and disciplined can provide a normative challenge to all moral theories in the spirit of Glaucon's perfectly unjust man, establishing and maintaining the appearances of morality, largely through highly visible general conformity, while discretely indulging in the most favorable opportunities. On the other hand, Nielsen's description of the life-long amoral alternative, due to the limitations of his uses of the key terms "being moral" and "being an amoral egoist," offers only a pathetic creature who is always immoral and selfish, entrenched in a life of misery that she brings upon herself and others. This latter description is not an appealing normative position, a weak alternative to morality, not at all in the spirit of Glaucon's challenge.

SELECTIVELY IMMORAL WITHOUT PERSISTENTLY SELFISH BEHAVIOR

In "Why Should I Be Moral? Revisited," the last chapter of *Why Be Moral?*, Nielsen argues that it is not necessarily irrational nor contrary to one's individual happiness to be what he calls an immoralist.[16]

> Will any person, no matter how he is placed in society, or what kind of society he is in, be unhappy, or at least less happy, than he otherwise would be, if he is an unprincipled bastard? Must an immoralist, anywhere, anytime, lead a life that he would find unsatisfying or at least less satisfying than the life he would have if he were not an immoralist? Plato and Aristotle think that he would. I will skeptically query that. I shall argue that no such general answer can be given as the one that Plato and Aristotle attempt to give. Whether an immoralist will be unhappy will depend on what kind of person he is, what kind of society he lives in, what his particular situation is in that society, and what kind of a self-image he has. Happiness no more necessarily requires morality than rationality does, though it can, in certain circumstances, be compatible with retaining firm moral commitments.[17]

Nielsen goes on to argue that it is a philosopher's myth that immorality never pays, that the immoralist is always secretly miserable.

It is in this article that Nielsen almost approaches describing an agent who can be immoral selectively like my personal amoral egoist.

> The immoralist can be selectively and prudently immoral—and this without a lot of rationalistic calculation. He need not be systematically or paranoidly immoral and, like Macbeth, drive everyone from him. Whether or not it is in your true interests to be moral depends on what sort of person you happen to be.[18]

Unfortunately, Nielsen does not go on to develop this idea of a purely self-interested agent who works selectively on personal gain through immoral actions. In fact, in speaking of the vulnerability of the immoralist who is an "individual egoist"[19] Nielsen writes,

> While many of us can and surely do get away with occasional thoroughly selfish and unprincipled acts, a deliberate, persistent policy of selfishness, even when it is intelligently cunning, is very likely to

bring on guilt feelings, punishment, estrangement from others as well as their contempt and hostility.[20]

In short, Nielsen is saying that a "persistent policy of selfishness" will not work, it will lose more than it will gain. For *most* selfish people, in the world as we know it, Nielsen is no doubt correct. However, part of the challenge of taking seriously the question "Why should I be moral rather than an amoral personal egoist?," like Glaucon's challenge, involves recognizing that (a) the systematic and selective egoistic life is not for everyone, and (b) as Glaucon puts it, "Nothing great is ever easy."

CAN THE PERSONAL EGOIST BECOME A GENUINE CRAFTSMAN?

In "Morality and Commitment" Nielsen suggests that the challenge of the "rational individual egoist" is really only a theoretical or academic possibility that really does not matter in daily life.

> ... the world being as it is and people being as they are, a rational individual egoist is very much like a unicorn: his existence is indeed possible but we do not expect to find him in our zoo; and such behavior is not the way to human happiness for flesh and blood individuals. But this remark is in no way a necessary proposition and it remains at least logically possible that some people might find not only a summer, but a life of happiness in this way .... Given the world and the people we find in it, the systematic rational egoist is a purely philosophic artifact.[21]

I disagree with Nielsen on this issue of empirical applicability of the idea of the personal egoist and its importance. People *trying* to be personal egoists can adversely affect the happiness of many others. People can act on the ideal of amoral personal egoism even if few people could ever lead the life without disastous self-defeating consequences, just like many people can try to play excellent golf although most competitors will remain "butchers" and crude turf movers.

Besides, these questions about the egoist, about what is possible and what can be achieved, are understood in light of the degree of sophistication and adaptability of the agent described. In the above quote, what is a "persistent policy of selfishness"? Does that include displaying selfish behavior even for satisfying short-sighted or trivial wants?

Of course, for the sophisticated amoral personal egoist, the whole idea of exhibiting behavior traits that are describable as selfish must be carefully eliminated as an everyday pattern within a systematic egoistic program.

No doubt one could overplay the "egoistic threat" either personally or politically, but discussion of *personal* egoism is very far from suffering from extreme emphasis, especially among philosophers who, as I have pointed out, have conceptually neglected it. If the amoral personal egoist is limited in her ability to "save appearances" or hide behind an illusory facade of virtue, what are these limitations and are these limitations a direct product of the nature of the egoist? And a related question is, can such limitations be overcome with simply greater finesse and technique? The undesirable consequences of egoism which Nielsen mentions, guilt feelings, punishment, and estrangement and hostility from others, are the kinds of things that an egoist can work on and potentially handle, especially an agent who can develop into a master of her craft. What is it about the amoral personal egoist that will produce what disastrous results? Perhaps there are consequences that follow systematically from being an amoral personal egoist that cannot be overcome by an expert "save the appearances" program. This is one of my main topics of Chapter Eight.

Simpler put, *the key question* is: is a genuine craftsman of the agency of the amoral personal egoist possible? Plato took that option seriously. So do I. Like Plato, if a true craftsman is not possible in this category of life, I expect an account explaining "Why not?" Like Glaucon, much of what I do through Chapter Seven in describing the amoral personal egoist is providing the setup, raising the level of discussion, so that these and related questions about the egoistic option, once properly clarified, can be treated with the seriousness that they deserve—given the world and its people as we know it.

Before leaving Nielsen's answer to "Why should I be moral?" let us focus on the form of his original argument. Nielsen argued that, given the moral and amoral alternatives, the choice of the amoral egoistic alternative as a consistent life-long policy is just disastrous to personal happiness. Nielsen's argument was weak because his description of the egoist was weak. But what if the characterization of the egoist is that of the enlightened, disciplined and selective egoist, rather than that of the predictably crude and repetitive immoralist? I suggest that a strong and interesting argument to consider is Nielsen's same argument with a more challenging egoist plugged in. The revised Nielsen argument then is the following: given what being an amoral personal egoist truly consists in, the conceptual development and practical maintenance of such an agency is disastrous to personal happiness. In Chapters Six and Seven of Part III, I will examine the conceptual and practical maintenance involved in really being such an amoral personal egoist. In Chapter Eight of Part IV, I will entertain the revised Nielsen argument as an answer to that fundamental question, that is based on the most interesting and challenging fundamental normative alternatives: Why should I be moral rather than an amoral personal egoist?

Thus far I have shown that the accounts of being moral by Sprigge and Nielsen fail to provide a specified option that is distinct from and not conceptually swallowed up by the concept of an enlightened amoral personal egoist. In each case an egoist could have chosen to be moral by either account of morality and yet remained a full-fledged amoral personal egoist. The option then, from the egoist's point of view anyway, of being an amoral egoist or being moral on the above two accounts of morality is really no genuine alternative at all; she can have it both ways, be the amoral egoist and be moral as well. The latter becomes but an egoistic conforming strategy applicable under certain conditions, rather than a fundamental normative alternative. In the case of the account of Kurt Baier, the attempt is made to establish moral reasons as superior reasons by appealing to a self-interested choice between two hypothetical worlds. No consideration is given to the first-person choice of an amoral personal egoist whose life goal is defined by his special role in a hypothetical world that he keeps to himself. Although Baier's account has its own variations, one can say that Sprigge, Baier, and Nielsen all fail to take the challenge of the amoral personal egoist seriously enough.

REDUCING MORAL THINKING
TO EGOISTIC THINKING

In sharp contrast to this all is the writing of Jesse Kalin. With Kalin's view, the fundamental alternative between being egoistic and being moral does not collapse because the former is underrated and therefore the latter is not sufficiently articulated as distinct. Rather with Kalin it is morality that is not taken seriously enough. The fundamental option collapses because Kalin simply attempts to reduce morality to egoism, to reduce moral thinking to a species of egoistic thinking. In the remainder of this chapter I discuss how Kalin attempts such a reduction, whether his reduction is successful, and most importantly what we can learn from Kalin's articulation of the options of being moral and being an amoral personal egoist and from his answer to the question, "Why should I be moral?"

Evidence of Kalin's desire to replace the moral option with egoism is his liberal use of those normative terms that are usually saved for morality, in the narrow sense of that institution whose normative guidelines for human action are attributed both interpersonal correctness and supreme authoritativeness. Kalin uses these moral terms in the very statement of his ethical egoism. The most glaring example of this sort of use appears at the very start of "In Defense of Egoism."

> Ethical egoism is the view that it is morally right—that is, morally permissible, indeed, morally obligatory—for a person to act in his own self-interest, even when his self-interest conflicts or is irreconcilable with the self-interest of another. The point people normally have in mind in accepting and advocating this ethical principle is that of justifying or excusing their own self-interested actions by giving them a moral sanction.[22]

Whether people "normally have in mind" the appeal to a moral sanction when they advocate Kalin's ethical egoism, who knows? We would have to first agree on what Kalin's ethical egoism is, find some people who advocate such, inquire about their motives, and then try to discover whether they are telling the truth. In any case, I find this combination of advocating egoism and seeking a moral sanction a strange one. Kant offers the reaction of common sense if such reason-giving were presented in person, rather than on the pages of contemporary philosophic literature:

> Suppose that an acquaintance whom you otherwise liked were to attempt to justify himself before you for having borne false witness by appealing to what he regarded as the holy duty of consulting his own happiness and, then, by recounting all the advantages he had gained thereby, pointing out the prudence he had shown in securing himself against detection, even by yourself, to whom alone he now reveals the secret only in order that he may be able at any time to deny it. And suppose that he then affirmed, in all seriousness, that he had thereby

fulfilled a true human duty—you would either laugh in his face or
shrink from him in disgust, even though you would not have the least
grounds for objecting to such measures if a man regulated his
principles solely with a view to his own advantage.[23]

Of course, whether one shares Kant's common sense in this
case will depend upon how one understands morality and how
seriously one takes it. In any case, it is important to recognize the
conceptual and normative options present behind the choice of
normative language in the philosophic presentation of normative
positions.

In his "Two Kinds of Moral Reasoning: Ethical Egoism as a
Moral Theory," Kalin replies to the objection that ethical egoism
cannot account for central features of morality. Key moves in
making his case that egoism can account for these features is Kalin's
subsuming morality under the category of egoistic activity, his
defining moral reasons as a subset of the more basic personal
(egoistic) reasons, and his treating the moral context as but a sub-
context of the situation in which the more fundamental activity of
personal reasoning takes place.

Kalin's reductive attempt begins with his distinction between
two kinds of moral reasoning, traditional reasoning and nontraditional or conventional reasoning. Traditional reasoning is the
activity of discovering moral principles or rules. Nontraditional
reasoning, illustrated by Kalin with the model of five boys deciding
the rules of a ball game,

> . . . is not the activity of discovery, but the activity of creation. It is the
> activity of establishing and adopting moral principles and moral rules.
> This activity is essential to their nature, existence, and correctness and
> hence is not simply the process by which they become known, for prior
> to or apart from this activity, they are not there to be known[24]

Kalin goes on to argue that there are only a few traditional
principles, that all of these are egoistic reasons, and that therefore,

> . . . unless nontraditional moral principles and reasons can be
> established using these egoistic ones as their basis, the only reasons in
> force in such cases, because the only traditional reasons available, will
> be egoistic ones.[25]

The only way that a nontraditional or conventional moral
principle can get established, according to Kalin, is by a Humean-
type mutual agreement of normative agents who each have

personal (i.e., egoistic) reasons to adopt mutually a system or institution of interpersonal reason-giving and regulating.

However, these nontraditional principles have a definite contingent status, for one can "avoid their force" by refusing to adopt an on-going system in the first place or by withdrawing from a previous agreement that one has made. Crucial to Kalin's egoistic account of morality is that it is rational, in the sense that one has reason, to "opt out" or "drop out" of this conventional institution one has entered whenever it is to one's overall self-interest to do so. But if this is so, it is difficult to understand in what sense one has entered an institution as a participant, on Kalin's account, as opposed to making use of a conventional tool that is handy without any genuine participation.

At the heart then of Kalin's reductionist account of morality lies the question, what does it mean to adopt these conventional or nontraditional principles, especially in light of this "opting out" feature? It is this "opting out" feature that adds an interesting complexity to any attempt to come to terms with Kalin's view that adopting morality can be like setting up the rules of five-boy baseball.

> The theory advanced by this paper is committed to saying of a person who had opted out of morality ... that the basic moral principles and rules have no force on him. He is not subject to them, just as persons in New York are not subject to Brazilian traffic laws.[26]

But just as one can avoid Brazilian traffic laws in New York City, one can travel in and out of Buffalo, New York, and Ontario Province, thereby altering the package of one's legal obligations. Although it is clear when a person physically leaves Buffalo, New York, and then she enters Ontario, it is not at all clear when one is *in* Kalin's hopscotch[27] system of morality and when one is *out*.

In the case of the amoral personal egoist there is no question about her straightforward approach to morality. She is an amoralist. As such she places no unqualified value on and makes no serious commitments to morality or any of its practices. She adopts nothing, other than, of course, her original egoistic imperative. If such an amoral personal egoist follows first-person constitutive rules or rules of thumb derivative from her egoistic imperative, she prescribes these for herself alone, as we discussed in Chapter Three. However, while she adopts no moral principles in a serious way, she may *make use of* all those practices that those other serious nonegoistic agents keep reinforcing. And the tide and flow of on-going conventional morality is both a factor to consider in egoistic calculation and a vehicle, if used carefully, for furthering her interests. But, to make use of what is available, for crowd control and psychological manipulation, is not to adopt a practice as seriously applying to oneself and others.

Now when we turn to Kalin's reductionist amoralism, everything is more cloudy. Instead of simply privately repudiating morality, while publicly handling its social consequences, as does the personal egoist, Kalin embraces the terminology of morality as a concerned loyalist, while the reformist package he offers just cannot account for the establishment of morality and its interpersonal reasoning and practices.

One could argue that Kalin's argument and attempted reduction of morality is just incomplete and has to be supplemented. On the crucial point of what it means to adopt a moral agreement, one might try to be helpful and ask the question: When or by what overt or symbolic act do we thereby officially adopt common moral systems when acting solely on personal, egoistic reasons? If one could stop the game of life and have everyone explicitly agree to a common set of interpersonal rules, such as all singing the national anthem before a sport event, then the theoretical mechanism of adopting is clear cut. But, similar to the problem of social contract theory in attempting to justify political obligations by appeal to the consent of the governed, the problem here is, in what does this adoption consist? The possibility of tacit adoption Kalin twice mentions, but does not discuss.[28] However, if one adopts interpersonal rules tacitly, how does one do this on Kalin's account, and furthermore, how does one opt out of a tacitly adopted rule? A related question is how do we know that all adopting participants are agreeing to the same set of rules and interpersonal reasons? If one can opt out of an adopted system of rules, cannot one adopt rules with X and Y exceptions in the first place? The problem then becomes, if the opting is done up front with exceptions initially built into the rules, how can one get from the agreements of a few "tribal moralities" to a larger universal morality?

The short of the problem is that Kalin's reductive account is not theoretically capable of answering such questions. It is not a case of adding what is needed to an incomplete ethical account.

The problem is that the kind of theory needed to account for morality can never be generated from Kalin's account of exclusively egoistic reason-giving. From his emphasis on individual creativity and complete flexibility in exclusively egoistic agreement-making, one cannot generate anything like genuine *participation* in an interpersonal moral system; on Kalin's account one can merely generate either (a) the temporary *use* of existing moral practices by a collection of egoistic agents or (b) the temporary agreements of cooperation between competing egoistic agents that are contingent upon the mutual recognition of de facto equality of power.[29]

To push Kalin's failure to account for morality one step further, let us consider what it would be like being a recipient of an agreement offer in Kalin's system. How does one know that the game announced and agreed to is in fact the only game being played and not part of a larger game of which one is not informed, such as watching new ball players fall into a six foot pit next to second base? Of course, if lying and deceit arise in one's moral "creations" ala Kalin, the injured recipient may want to say that "Lying is wrong." But what would that mean in Kalin's system of conventional adoptions of rules for exclusively egoistic reasons? Can it only mean something like, "Lying is at this time a procedure that I do not want to be chosen in our interpersonal agreements," perhaps adding "I hope that you will not start to lie or continue to lie at this time"?

As a spectator from the outside looking onto Kalin's ball field, one may say that it is just not fair to make an agreement when one is "just passing through" the moral ball field ready to opt out of what one has just adopted. However, a primitive moral notion like fairness or goodwill takes on but an instrumental value within Kalin's system. Kalin defines good will as a contingent trade-off in self-seeking based upon a reciprocal recognition of equality of power:

> The conclusion to be drawn is that morality rationally rests on one or both of two conditions—general good will and equality of power. In the case of good will, the moral relations are themselves of personal value.... However, such acceptance is rational only if it is shared. Failing reciprocation, the institutional equality characterizing morality can be based only on equality of power, which in the final analysis will be the power of hurting one another, that is, of adversely affecting each other's interests.[30]

But is this treatment of such moral concepts at all surprising in an account of morality that makes morality a subset of egoism?

On the last page of "Two Kinds of Moral Reasoning," Kalin gives us a bit more insight into what he wants to replace morality with and why. In the same paragraph in which he talks of a "correct understanding of morality," Kalin says his egoistic theory

> ... begins, rather, with a desire to avoid what it senses as an irreparable loss, the sacrifice of one's life or interests to the interests of others, and with the Kantian (and not Platonic) question about this desire, "What is the most reasonable thing for me to do in this situation?[31]

So at the heart of this "correct understanding of morality" is reasoning based upon the fear of sacrificing one's life or personal interests. In sharp contrast to this way of thinking about the role of sacrificing one's own interests is the thinking of Plato's Socrates in the *Apology*. Socrates warns us that,

> ... in every kind of danger there are plenty of devices for avoiding death if you are unscrupulous enough to stick at nothing. But I suggest, gentlemen, that the difficulty is not so much to escape death; the real difficulty is to escape from doing wrong, which is far more fleet of foot.[32]

Of course, Socrates would argue that the only irreparable losses are not what Kalin fears but the moral harms that one inflicts upon oneself by one's moral choices. Whether or not Socrates is right that moral crime never pays, because it harms the most essential part of oneself, one's soul, the fact is that Socrates unlike Kalin is concerned about sacrificing a different kind of good, moral good. And Socrates is reminding us that there is a distinct form of reasoning about what is right and wrong that cannot be reduced to the efficacy of attaining this personal good or avoiding that personal danger.

Turning again to the words of F. H. Bradley,

> For morality ... teaches us that, if we look on her only as good for something else, we never in that case have seen her at all. ... Degrade her, and she disappears; and to keep her, we must love and not merely use her.[33]

With what can Kalin reply in correcting our understanding on these matters? Perhaps that morality has not disappeared but has been given a radical face lift. Or perhaps that she did disappear but we need not miss her, for the mannequin of egoistic conventionalism will be just as *useful* on center stage in the practical arena.

Although thinly veiled by his confusing use of moral terms and by his implication about reforming those non-egoistic ideas that we moralists share, it is clear that Kalin offers his readers a qualitatively different replacement for the theory and practice of morality.

I suggest, but will not pursue this line of argument here, that the most central and basic feature in explaining the phenomenon of morality is the master concept that orders the normative thinking of the moral agent, such that she views herself and every other human agent as the same kind of agent participating in a common procedure for evaluating one's thought and practice. Now, as I will discuss more carefully in Chapters Six and Seven, to understand the genuine egoist, one must understand the unique conceptual perspective with which the egoist views herself vis-a-vis all other normative agents. One reply to Kalin is that, if one talks fundamental features of morality, one must also talk key organizing concepts or master concepts. And to try to explain the master concept of a normative agent like Plato's Socrates in the *Apology* using only the conceptual unity and orientation of an amoral egoist, or a whole community of egoists busily manipulating each other, is absurd.

RELATIVISTIC BASIS OF KALIN'S REDUCTION

Before completing my evaluation of Kalin's reductive attempt, it is important to point out his heavy reliance upon relativism. In his 1975 article "Two Kinds of Moral Reasoning," Kalin is explicit regarding the relativistic basis for his avoiding the charges of logical inconsistency. Kalin argues that his critics are mistaken on this point because the ethical egoist's "ought"-statements do not have the same implications as do the "ought"-statements of us non-egoists; the implications are different because the logical structure is different, and the unique logical structure of egoism is due to its relativistic base. Kalin puts it this way:

> I shall use "a" to refer to direct ought-statements of the form 'M ought to do X in S' and "B" to refer to ought-statements of the form 'It ought to be the case that M do X in S.' Any system of reasons in which an a-statement implies a B-statement is a strong system of reasons, and any in which a-statements do not imply B-statements is a weak system.

... ethical egoism is a weak system in which its ought-statements have no B-consequences ... .

Weak systems, where one cannot infer from a-statements to any B-statements at all, do not imply that there is anything that ought to be the case ... . In such systems, the fact that M may have conclusive reasons for doing X in S ('ought, all things considered') does not mean that X or anything else ought to be done ... .

This means that weak systems must have a different logical structure, and therefore a different foundation, than strong systems. In particular, they cannot include any B-statements which are independently grounded. Rather they must presuppose relativistic values and reasons which are dependent on person-specific characteristics such as the agent's wants and interests.[34]

Kalin avoids logical inconsistency by shrinking the logical field of play with his new structure of reasoning. He is saying something like, "Yes, I would have such logical difficulties if I opted for the same traditional reasoning about 'ought'-judgments, but that is an area of the ball field in which I do not care to play; and, furthermore, to legitimize my uniqueness, I hereby create a set of rules of play that permits logical maneuvers only within very limited boundaries." However, the theoretical price that Kalin pays for his rewriting the rules of play is an expensive one in the area of common ground with other moral philosophers and in the area of the overall clarity of his position.

However, even more damaging to Kalin is the fact that his relativism can be turned upon his own arguments. If weak systems like Kalin's ethical egoism presuppose relativistic values and reasons dependent upon person-specific characteristics, is not the reasoning by the defender of such a weak system itself dependent on theorist-specific characteristics? Is he claiming his theory is true or is it only true for himself, the author of "Two Kinds of Moral Reasoning?" Does it make any sense to talk of the merit or success of Kalin's argument if it is all relative to this one theorist only?

If one pushes this relativistic aspect of Kalin's view, some strange consequences appear. Although his theory is nominally universal, if the valid applicability of the view is limited to himself alone, why should anyone else care about it? Similarly, given this relativism, why should Kalin himself have any concern over whether we non-egoistic types think his egoism is logically incoherent or whether his egoism can account for the thinking and practice of morality, a completely different game of meanings and reasoning? And, if Kalin can claim only that ethical egoism is right for him (alone), then to say, as does Kalin, that it is a possible moral view is very uninteresting and as such is not deserving of "... extensive argumentation involving features at the very heart of ethics."

When Kalin talks more ambitiously to the effect that "... egoism can in fact serve as the foundation of morality" and the gain to be had from Kalin's account is "a correct understanding of morality," is he saying that this is true or a correct understanding of morality? Or, on the other hand, is he proposing a new model for thinking about morality? If the latter, for what end? Is he merely suggesting that this model of thinking is personally expedient for each of his readers,[35] in the sense that it would be in the interest of each person to think in this fashion? This expediency model is very suspect on grounds of workability, and in fact may produce a life for each that is "nasty, brutish, and short."

Similarly, when Kalin concludes that, because nature provides a "prejudicial distribution" of interests and resources, "... we must choose between the ethical and the moral, and reason is now on the side of the ethical,"[36] is he not implying that it is, at least now, more rational to be an ethical egoist or that the best reasons support being an ethical egoist? But what can this mean given his relativistic methodological tools? He could be saying that he alone has opted for the egoistic side. But if so, why should anyone else opt for his reasons? To say that Kalin opts that others should also so opt does not get one very far. Kalin has the strange task of trying to communicate intellectual appeal over a relativistic wall that he has defensively built around his theory.

What Kalin wants to say about egoism and morality over-reaches what he can effectively and consistently defend given the theoretical tools he has chosen. Brian Medlin charged that, "I'm a philosopher, not a rat catcher, and I don't see it as my job to dig vermin out of such burrows as individual egoism."[37] To extend Medlin's analogy, it looks as though what Kalin is trying to do is to drag the egoist out of his burrow and dress him up respectable-like for philosophers. The problem is that the theoretical clothing with which Kalin dresses the egoist just does not fit and in fact causes him to trip when he tries to advance in more than one direction.

I summarize my fourth chapter discussion: We have learned that to understand the question "Why should I be moral?" as a genuine question of practical importance requires an appreciation of *both* the agency of the personal amoral egoist and the agency of the moralist, as clearly distinct from the former. We have learned that the question is a survivor. When one attempts to eliminate the question by definition or at one level, it surfaces again at a more basic level. For example, when Kalin attempts to define morality out of the ethical picture, the question remains "Why be egoistic— in the first place, rather than the other genuine alternative, being moral? Similarly, we learned that one cannot assume away the "Why should I be moral?" question by accepting only some kinds of reasons; for the question of accepting exclusively which kinds of first-person reasons must wait upon the more basic question about being the kind of normative agent who respects and gives certain kinds of reasons.

We have also learned that the interesting question about being moral or not is a question about being a certain kind of agent, a question of agent morality; the interesting question is not about mere behavior conformity. The real egoist provides an authentic challenge to morality in the spirit of Plato's Glaucon. She is not a straw man. She is not a crude non-conforming immoralist who sticks out like a sore thumb in society. She sets her own rules of behavior based on her egoistic imperative and on the evaluation of her abilities for success in relevant situations. She judges each question of conformity to current moral norms in the same way, as simply an egoistic calculation in light of all estimated effects on human obstacles and resources.

We have also been reminded by the evaluation of Kalin's view that the authentic egoist does not allow herself to get involved in the meta-ethical defense of her egoism: to do so is self-defeating *qua* egoist, to be a bungler on Plato's account. Rather, following Glaucon's account of the perfectly unjust man, the clever amoral personal egoist, displaying her mastery of her craft, will carefully maintain her secrecy and take account of the consequences of her actions.

Notes

[1] T. L. S. Sprigge, "Definition of a Moral Judgment," in G. Wallace and A. D. M. Walker, eds., *The Definition of Morality* (London: Methuen & Co., Ltd., 1970), p. 130.

2 For Kant's discussion of the merchant with a "direct inclination" to act in accordance with duty, see Immanual Kant's *Groundwork of the Metaphysic of Morals*, p. 65.

3 Baier, *The Moral Point of View*, p. 27.

4 Ibid., p. 28.

5 Ibid., p. 28, emphasis is Baier's.

6 Ibid., p. 150.

7 Ibid., pp. 150-51.

8 For similar criticism of Baier's argument in terms of Thomas Nagel's distinction between "agent-relative reasons" and "agent-neutral reasons," see Kai Nielsen's "Must the Immoralist Act Contrary to Reason?" in his *Why be Moral?* esp. pp. 279-83.

Nielsen writes, "Baier's ethical rationalism commits him to the view that agent-neutral reasons are overriding or superior reasons, but he has given us no adequate grounds for believing that they are ... . But Baier has not shown why or even that a clear understanding of her world (including her own situation) always requires *an agent* to adopt that perspective ... . When the immoralist deliberately lets certain agent-relative reasons override agent-neutral reasons, she need not in any way be acting contrary to reason."

The above Nielsen article is a response to the following two more recent Baier articles: "The Conceptual Link Between Morality and Rationality," *Nous* 7 (1982) and "Rationality, Reason, and the Good" in David Copp and David Zimmerman (eds.) *Morality, Reason and Truth* (Totowa, N.J/: Rowman and Allanheld, 1985), pp. 193-211.

9 Hospers, *Human Conduct*, p. 194.

10 Nielsen,"Why Should I Be Moral?" in his *Why Be Moral?*, p. 181.

11 Ibid., p. 186.

12 Ibid., p. 192.

13 "Point of Morality" in *Reason and Practice*, p. 318.

14 Ibid., p. 315.

15 Nielsen, "Why Should I Be Moral?" p. 193.

16 This term "immoralist" is a challenging one in terms of clarity. Nielsen uses the term to at least mean a person who is willing to be immoral to further her

own interest. Why Nielsen chooses to distinguish this kind of agent from purely an amoral egoist I will discuss in Chapter Five along with Nielsen's account of the "classist immoralist."

[17] Nielsen, "Why Should I Be Moral? Revisited," in *Why Be Moral?*, p. 292.

[18] Ibid., p. 294. Nielsen is using "systematically" in this passage to mean "continually, all the time" unlike my own use of the term in talking about the personal egoist who is systematically egoistic at the same time she is selectively immoral within that egoistic system.

[19] Nielsen uses the term "individual egoist" here, rather than "personal egoist." I prefer saving the former term for one who has a *theory* that guides *everyone* to further the individual egoist's self-interest. The personal egoist, as I have been using the term throughout, would be better used here, the theory-for-everyone aspect of individual egoism is not at issue here at all.

[20] Ibid., p. 297.

[21] Nielsen, "Morality and Commitment" in his *Why Be Moral?*, pp. 197-98.

[22] Jesse Kalin, "In Defense of Egoism," in David P. Gauthier, ed., *Morality and Rational Self-Interest* (Englewood Cliffs, N.J.: Prentice Hall, 1970), p. 69.

[23] Kant, *Critique of Practical Reason*, p. 36.

[24] Kalin, "Two Kinds of Moral Reasoning: Ethical Egoism as a Moral Theory," *Canadian Journal of Philosophy* 5 (1975), p. 324.

[25] Ibid., p. 327.

[26] Ibid., p. 338.

[27] In reading about Kalin's "adopt in" and "opt out" features of morality, I could not get out of my mind this picture of moral error as illustrated by the analogy of a clumsy child, who has just completed her turn at hopscotch, and who then turns around and tries to explain *post facto* why she chose to hop in which squares and for what reasons.

[28] Ibid., on page 333 Kalin mentions parenthetically "usually tacit"; on page 334, also parenthetically, he mentions "at least tacit."

[29] Compare these very fragile and changing conditions for agreement with John Rawls' contractual situation in his delineation of justice as fairness. "In justice as fairness the original position of equality ... is understood as a purely hypothetical situation characterized so as to lead to a certain conception of justice. Among the essential features of this situation is that no

one knows his place in society, ... his intelligence, strength, and the like ... . The principles of justice are chosen behind a veil of ignorance." *A Theory of Justice* (Cambridge, Mass.: Harvard University Press, 1971), p. 12.

[30] Kalin, "Two Kinds of Moral Reasoning," p. 339.

[31] Ibid., p. 355.

[32] Plato, *Apology* in Hugh Tredennick, ed., *The Last Days of Socrates* (Baltimore: Penguin Books, Inc., 1969), p. 73.

[33] Bradley, "Why Should I Be Moral?," p. 3.

[34] Kalin, "Two Kinds of Moral Reasoning," pp. 341-42.

[35] Again, the practical inconsistency question, what reason would an "enlightened" egoist have for sharing the egoistic news with "naive" non-egoists, whether philosophers or not? By contrast, if the real egoist published on morality, would she not focus on propping up conventional morality; why?—so that it is easy to work the crowd on a sunny day.

[36] Ibid., p. 355. Kalin's use of "the ethical" here, as opposed to "the moral," can be understood as simply the egoistic point of view, for he equates ethical reasons with egoistic reasons, as part of his egoistic reduction.

[37] Medlin, "Ultimate Principles and Ethical Egoism," p. 59.

Chapter Five

Is the Personal Egoist a Club Member?

In this chapter I raise some questions about the relation between my description of the amoral personal egoist and the egoist's membership in groups. Given my claim that *personal egoism* is the only form of egoism that measures up to the amoral challenge of "Why should I be moral?", what does this form of egoism imply about the egoist's joining groups and maintaining her membership in groups? Is there anything special about the personal amoral egoist's membership in groups? Can a *personal* amoral egoist even join groups at all?

I will sketch a brief answer to these and similar questions in light of my description of the amoral personal egoist. Then I will present three objections to my argument of the first four chapters, each objection having to do with the personal nature of my egoistic account and the special challenges of egoistic group membership. The heart of the chapter will be my evaluation of these three objections. The product of these analyses and evaluations will be a further clarification of the amoral personal egoist's position and further defense of my claim that this position comprises a strongest-case analysis of an amoral challenge that is truly egoistic at the fundamental level.

For the amoral personal egoist the matter of joining groups is not problematic, she simply joins those groups of human resources which provide the most potential for satisfying her prioritized wants, including her long-range goals. As discussed in Chapter Three, one of her concerns, of course, is maintaining secrecy and not revealing herself as the agent she is. Accordingly, she may avoid those groups and group activities which involve sharing with others about herself and her thoughts. In order to avoid the needless complexity of introducing additional adjustment cover-up activities, she may keep most of her thoughts about herself to herself simply to keep her life simpler and more manageable. In short, with due concern for maintaining a secrecy about her personal egoism, she only joins those groups which it is egoistically efficient for her to be a member of, given her prioitized wants.

One kind of group she will *not* be joining is an *egoistic* group at the fundamental level. As an amoral *personal* egoist, she works alone *as an egoist.* She, of course, makes use of her human resources, individually and in groups, on an everyday basis whenever they are needed. Yet, in so far as she remains egoistically efficient, she will base all her activites, plans and interactions with others upon her fundamental egoistic principle that specifies furthering *exclusively* her interests regardless of others. At the categorical level, she prescribes for herself alone. She may help others or accommodate others or even sacrifice in some sense for others if and only if such moves are indirectly beneficial to furthering her interests which at bottom are the only ones she counts.

GROUPS OF PERSONAL EGOISTS

The first of three objections to my argument I call the *descriptive group* objection. If there is more than one of these personal egoists scheming around (they do not have to know about each other, they do not even have to be good at it, some or even all can even be bunglers), then so called personal egoism is not a theory for one person only; it is a group theory about a subset of human beings who value, plan and think of others in a like way.

Consider the following thought experiment: An "egometer" is invented which is capable of detecting by surveilance that special combination of thought patterns, self-talk, planning, PR activities and manipulation which specially characterizes the personal egoist. Let us say that in a given geographic region the egometer registers three personal egoists. Let us assume further the egometer is 100% accurate. No matter if neither egoist A nor B nor C is aware that any of the others are personal egoists, no matter how effective each of these characters are at deceiving one another and hiding their personal egoistic character behind the facade of "illusory virtue," the egometer reader knows that she has a group of three personal egoists at work on each other (perhaps) and other people.

Do we no longer then have a personal egoism theory for one person only but now a theory about a *group* of egoists? Is it a mistake to even talk about a personal egoist with a normative position for one person only? Once one has more than one of these characters, the theory goes, then one has a group theory, not a personal theory.[1]

My reply to this objection is that it confuses the *descriptive* group categorization of similar agents with the *normative* position of the amoral personal egoist. The former activity places agents within a group in order to classify them in light of de facto similar features of their agency. In ethics, normative positions and normative theories have different purposes than simply classifying and describing by groups. They are prescriptive, action-guiding. The amoral personal egoist's normative position[2] is defined in light of the egoist's fundamental prescription, what she basically *ought* to do, the most fundamental practical principle which should guide (in fact does, if she is efficient) all her practical decisions and her complete practical life. As the holder of a *normative* position, the amoral personal egoist, as I have defined her, can indeed and does have a normative position for one person only, although she can also in fact be classified as a member of a group of similar agents.

This important difference between accepting a classifying description and holding a normative principle at the fundamental level can be easily confused if one does not take the amoral personal egoist's *amorality* seriously. If one thinks of morality as a guideline for everyone (or at least most people) and egoism as a substitute for morality, then it is easy to view egoism as a similar "big group project" that can be similarly described as morality is described. But to think in this rough way is to miss the very special character of the amoral egoist's position.

As an amoralist, amoral personal egoist A rejects the thinking and practices of morality as any real guide at all in her life. She recognizes its social benefits, even for herself, and she plans to take advantage of its importance in the lives of her human resources, but taking advantage of an on-going practice is a different matter from sharing a commitment to a common system of interpersonal evaluation. In the complete absence then of any moral system that is recognized by her as validly applying to her, this egoistic amoralist cleans the slate and begins anew, as the moral outlaw, not trying to redo or replace any group system or set of

practices but to prescribe for herself alone a fundamental egoistic
principle that does not apply to any other person.

Does this amoral personal egoist A have the *identical
normative theory* as egoist B (assuming that B rejects, commits,
prescribes and organizes her practical life in the same basic kind of
way as A)? I argue that she does *not*. Egoists A and B are not
sharing the same theory in common, any more than CIA and KGB
intelligence officers are all part of the same intelligence system. It
is no doubt correct to classify both the CIA and KGB officers as
doing the same *kind* of work, in so far as they both gather
intelligence. But note that to *completely* describe what each does is
to include the crucial difference between their work, that one spies
for the USA and the other for the former Soviet Union, they do *not*
do the exact same thing, but a similar kind of job.

So too the respective normative positions of amoral personal
egoists A and B can be correctly but incompletely described as
both egoistic positions of the same kind. But, as with the spies, the
amoral personal egoists are not doing the exact same thing nor are
they sharing the same theory in a more precise sense. The
normative position of each agent A and B is based upon separate
fundamental, normative egoistic principles, each of which is
referenced to the egoist who prescribes it at the categorical level,
i.e., "I ought to further my own self-interest and disregard ... ."

In summary, the true egoist who is both amoral and a personal
egoist prescribes and endorses an egoism which is applied to
herself alone and, in so far as she is systematic and consistent, upon
which she builds and evaluates her entire life and its activities.
Although others may classify the amoral personal egoist as holding
the same kind of theory as others, the egoist's commitment and
loyalty is to herself alone in light of her fundamental egoistic
principle. The true personal egoist with the clean slate of the
amoralist could care less about how others classify her kind, could
care less about the sophisticated comparisons made possible by
the new egometer, as long as the egometer's inventor stays in his
laboratory. But once the inventor turns informant, the egoist may
ridicule him to silence or perhaps take him out with a cruise
missile—whatever it takes, given her fundamental normative
principle. However the ethics books may label and classify her, to
the amoral personal egoist herself, given her normative position,
the only relevant agent categories are herself and her resources.

PLATO'S SECRET SOCIETIES

The second objection arises out of attention to Plato's own Book II dialogue. After Adeimantus considers the objection that it is not always easy to hide vice, he replies that "nothing great is easy," and then goes on to state that one of the key ways to maintain secrecy is by forming groups of fellow cohorts of injustice:

> To remain undiscovered we'll form secret societies and political clubs. And there are teachers of persuasion to make us clever in dealing with assemblies and law courts. Therefore, using persuasion in one place and force in another, we'll outdo others without paying a penalty.[3]

The objection is, if Plato's amoralism is basically a group amoralism, then perhaps the amoralism that I have been describing should likewise be revised to a group position of some sort, following Plato's model. Since Plato's amoralism is indeed a group program, this account of the amoral personal egoist should be revised to a group amoralist position as well.

Although there is some tension between the emphasis on the individual and the group in Glaucon and Adeimantus' amoralist challenge, I argue that Plato's amoralism is basically a challenge about the unjust *individual* amoralist. Secondly, I argue that the amoralist in a group, "secret society or political club," has only tentative loyalty to the group balancing on the thin edge of de facto estimates of power, and therefore it is not fundamentally a group amoralism at all. Thirdly, so-called group amoralism has some of the same clarification and definition problems as does universal egoism which we discussed in Chapter Three. It really makes no sense to talk about a group amoralist *at the fundamental level.*

In the Glaucon-Adeimantus account there is no question that the amoralist becomes a member of some groups; the crucial question is, what is the status of these group memberships? There is one other passage in the Glaucon-Adeimantus amoralist challenge in which the individual person is discussed in conjunction with a group of others. Glaucon says that a complete description of the unjust man must include how, like a clever craftsman,

> If he happens to slip, he must be able to put it right. If any of his unjust activities should be discovered, he must be able to speak persuasively or to use force. And if force is needed, he must have the help of courage and strength and of the substantial wealth and friends with which he has provided himself.[4]

In this passage and context Glaucon is talking about an individual unjust person. Friends, like wealth, personal courage and strength, and the ability to speak persuasively, are spoken of here as things with which the individual amoralist "has provided himself." Clearly, it is amoralism from an individual point of view that is here at issue.

In Adeimantus' passage about "forming secret societies and political clubs" Plato moves to a dramatic first-person plural[5] response to the objection, "... it isn't easy for vice to remain always hidden."

> We'll reply that nothing great is easy. And, in any case, if we're to be happy, we must follow the path indicated in these accounts. To remain undiscovered we'll form secret societies and political clubs.[6]

The accounts which Adeimantus refers to in the above quote refer to all the sayings, stories, descriptions of attitudes and arguments about how the unjust person's actions are more profitable and how her injustice is "fixed" or covered over in all kinds of ways with the appearance of (illusory) virtue. The path we must follow, Adeimantus writes, if we (distributively-each one of us) want to be happy, is for each of us to be systematically unjust (an individual amoralist) but secure a reputation for justice and maneuver to keep that facade working for one, since "opinion forcibly overcomes truth" and "controls happiness." Plato gives no better description of this path than the following:

> I should create a facade of illusory virtue around me to deceive those who come near, but keep behind it the greedy and crafty fox of the wise Archilochus.[7]

To get at the status of the amoralist's group membership in the Glaucon-Adeimantus account, a *key question* is what can be the only reason for maintaining one's group membership in "secret societies and political clubs"? For a morality-respecting agent, there are various applicable reasons for staying in a group, contributing to it, etc., such as (a) you gave your word, (b) that is only fair, (c) to do so would produce the greatest amount of happiness for the group, or (d) to do so is the way that you and others can continue to flourish in noble ways as human beings. But given the amoralism of the Glaucon-Adeimantus account, all these reasons for group loyalty which we morality-respecting agents take for granted are simply not applicable. Justice on the account under examination is but a poor compromise among people too weak to do injustice with impunity, to live the most profitable life. However, the only motivating reason for doing the just thing on this account is also because it is profitable, it pays, it furthers the interest of each participant given the limitations in power and ability. Doing the just thing then is a reluctant second choice, an inferior option to using one's ability and power to be unjust without having to compromise.

On the Glaucon-Adeimantus amoralist account then the only reason for being *unjust* is profit, furthering one's self-interest. And the only reason for being *just* is the same, profit or self-interest. All just reasons, all moral reasons, are reduced on this account also to self-interested efficiency reasons. It is a mistake to characterize Plato's amoralism as a group amoralism, as if loyal members of these societies or clubs are "all in this together" in some common normative unity. The only amoralism here is individual amoralism because the only recognized reasons for action are self-interested reasons, without any common background system of evaluation. The only motivation for these individualistic amoralists to come together in groups is to manipulate one another and deceive to a higher degree all those who do not have the courage or intelligence to join their secret groups.

But make no mistake, on this account these "enlightened" groups are only *tentative* and *temporary* groupings which work together only for so long as they are of mutual benefit and so long as there remain similar estimates by all members of a de facto equality of power, or an equal impotence for real power, the power to be unjust with impunity.

The best way to characterize these "secret societies and political clubs" is as groups of *individual self-interested amoralists* who *each*, for the life of each soon-to-change group, creates a facade of illusory group loyalty around herself to deceive (or at least keep off guard) all others within the group, while *each* at the same time keeps behind this phoney facade a "greedy and crafty fox" with interests only in self. The "foxes" stay together as a group only so long as the power estimates are within the same parameters. As Adeimantus puts it,

> ... apart from someone of godlike character who is disgusted by injustice or one who has gained knowledge and avoids injustice for that reason, no one is just willingly. Through cowardice or old age or

some other weakness, people do indeed object to injustice. But it's obvious that they do so only because they lack the power to do injustice, for the first of them to acquire it is the first to do as much injustice as he can.[8]

Therefore, a close look at Plato's amoral challenge in the *Republic*'s Book II gives no reasons to alter the *personal* amoralist (and egoistic) account that I have been clarifying, for at bottom Plato's account like mine is developed from a thoroughly single-individual point of view.

Note the similar clarity problem that the so-called "group amoralist" shares with the universal egoist. We showed in Chapter Three that the universal egoist cannot successfully *be* what she claims to be, that it is not at all clear what it even means to adopt universal egoism as one's primary, unqualified normative commitment. Similarly, what is a "group amoralist"? If the term "group amoralist" only means an amoralist in a group, like a puddle amoralist could mean an amoralist in a puddle, then the term "group amoralist," if not a complete oxymoron, is just not helpful for ethics.

CLASSIST IMMORALIST

The third objection to my argument of the first four chapters comes from Kai Nielsen's last chapter of *Why Be Moral?* Nielsen writes that what he calls the *classist immoralist* position is a stronger challenge to the authority of morality than the positions of the personal or individual egoist. If Nielsen is correct, then my interpretation of "Why should I be moral?" featuring the amoral personal egoist cannot be a strongest-case analysis of the question.

Nielsen argues that the classist immoralist position is the stronger position because (a) it is not as vulnerable to negative consequences (guilt feelings, punishment, estrangement and hostility) as is egoistic immoralism and (b) it provides more security in life in making available sources of comfort and happiness. Part of the challenge of evaluating Nielsen's classist immoralist is that the position is not clearly stated; a case can be made that it amounts to *either* a rather crude limited version of the flexible amoral personal egoist *or* a strange mix of selective moral and egoistic elements within an unappealing, unreflecting agent who arbitrarily appeals to emotivism and subjectivism as convenient. After laying out Nielsen's position as best I can, I will argue that if the classist immoralist does not simply reduce to an in-the-closet amoral personal egoist, then the position remains conceptually confusing, is loaded with ethical theory problems, and at the same time greatly underestimates the practical consequences of holding such a position.

To get a handle on Nielsen's key concept, I begin by explaining the generic immoralist. The immoralist according to Nielsen is one who is willing to and in fact does (selectively, if she is smart) what she recognizes to be wrong (immoral) in pursuit of her long-term interest.

> Can it be shown that, no matter who I am, ... my long-term self-interest is more likely to be satisfied if I, in conjunction with everyone else ... am doing what morally speaking is the right thing to do, than, if everybody else or even (perhaps) most people are so acting, and I, undetected, am not so acting? Must a prudent intelligent immoralist make himself unhappy or harm even his own long-term self-interest by continuing to be such an immoralist?
>
> Such an at least putatively rational immoralist will be an adroit free-rider ... . He will, if he is thoroughly rational and reflective, want others to restrict their exclusive pursuit of their self-interest. But what he reflectively wants for himself is another matter.[9]

Nielsen is very close in this passage to defining the immoralist as simply a personal egoist. He is just about there if he goes on and makes explicit that Nielsen's immoralist's pursuit of her self-interest is an *exclusive* pursuit in the sense of *regardless* of the welfare and interests of others, if attending to these things does not pay for the immoralist.[10] On the other hand, Nielsen could have explicitly eliminated the option of the exclusive-pursuit interpretation of the generic immoralist by simply defining the immoralist as pursuing her self-interest (period), leaving open the possibility that the immoralist can have moral reasons some of the time and genuine respect for some people, as well as self-interested reasons.

As I showed in Chapter Four, Nielsen underestimates the purely egoistic agent, what Nielsen calls the individual egoistic immoralist. I will not repeat that discussion here but it is relevant to Nielsen's comparative argument that classist immoralism is a stronger position. The master of the craft of egoism need not remain vulnerable to but can handle potential guilt feelings, the threats of punishment, and estrangement and hostility—such challenges simply come with the territory.

Nielsen's second argument emphasizing the weakness of the individual egoist's position is that she cannot have "securely available" to her "… companionship, love, approval, security and recognition."[11] On the contrary, I argue that the egoist who has developed her personal and social skills and who understands people can securely obtain all of these human goods, including friendships of utility and pleasure (following Aristotle's groupings) and many kinds of love. The only kind of love that the egoist cannot obtain, as I discuss in Chapter Eight, is love based on genuine friendship. In fact, there is not in principle any reason why the egoist cannot be loved genuinely for long periods of time by nonegoistic, other-regarding and devoted people. Of course, egoistic secrecy is crucial here and all such intimate interpersonal maneuvering may be very challenging, not everyone could do it, but again such a life is "not for everyone." That is part of the challenge for the amoral personal egoist.

Of course, if one shackles the potential of the egoistic mind and the egoistic lifestyle by characterizing the egoist as always having very socially readable behavior that is continually selfish in its treatment of others, then the consequences of being an egoist will be such that she drives people away, achieves no social respect, and pays the resulting prices of uncomfortable living. But then, the egoist need not be a self-defeating bungler who keeps shooting herself in the foot.[12]

I turn now in Nielsen's argument from the weaknesses of the individual egoistic option of the immoralist to the strengths of the classist kind of immoralist. Nielsen defines the latter term in the following way:

> I mean by "a classist amoralist" (a) a person who is part of the dominant elite in such a society, (b) a person who only extends his disinterested caring to his own peers and to those underlings (servants, mistresses and the like) he just happens to care about, and (c) a person who treats all other people manipulatively, deploying morality as moral ideology to keep those people in line in such a way that the interests of his class, and with that his own interests, are furthered. He has genuine moral relations with his peers—the members of the elite class. Between such people there can be genuine love, disinterested concern, justice: the genuine reciprocities that partly constitute morality; but this is not extended, by the classist amoralists in that elite, to their relations with the vast dominated class. They, or at least most of them, are treated manipulatively. For them, our classist amoralist believes, moral ideology with its artful semblance of morality is enough. The thing to

do with them, he avers, is, with the adroit use of the consciousness industry, to do a real snow job on them. But there is for the classist amoralist no question of treating them morally as equal members of a Kantian kingdom of ends. An artful disguise of morality is all that is required or desirable from the perspective of his classist amoralism.[13]

Nielsen argues that the classist immoralist's position is much stronger than that of the individual egoist immoralist because the former agent need not be restricted to self-serving reason-giving or self-serving relationships.

> They may within their class have reciprocal relationships which are not at all self-serving—let alone "ultimately self-serving." Indeed, if they did not have such non-self-interested reasons, they would suffer at least some of the vulnerabilities of egoists, for friendship and love would not, at least in their full senses, be available to them. It is an essential requirement of friendship that one desires the other's happiness and welfare regardless of self-serving purposes. But the classist amoralist can, at least within his class, have such full-fledged relationships. He is an immoralist not because he is an egoist; he is an immoralist because he is quite willing deliberately to treat members of the other classes as means only, as people to be manipulated and used to further either or both his individual interests or the interests of his class, regardless of the consequences to those people who are members of the dominated class ... . He keeps his caring and respect within his own class and only occasionally and selectively does he let it extend to some other people. And then it is an extension not based on moral grounds but on liking. He extends his moral concern to people he comes in close contact with and just happens to come to care for.[14]

At first look, Nielsen's classist immoralist appears to be the point of view of an agent with a partitioned ethical program, which treats members of her own dominant social class as full-fledged moral agents while treating all other people amorally, as outsiders to the moral domain, as instruments to be manipulated. The status of the members of the unfortunate dominated class is very clear. But the status of the domain of moral agents within the partitioned program is not clear.

Many questions about moral theory arise, *if* one treats the classist immoralist position as if it were simply a system divided solely by class. What justification can be given for restricting morality is this way? Can one in this system make valid moral judgments across class divisions? For example, does it make sense to ask, is it right (morally) for members of the dominated class to steal from the dominant class? (Of course, what is said to the exploited class, "a real snow job" perhaps, is another matter, a different question altogether.)   All the consistency questions relevant to the nationalist or racist positions wait in the wings on Nielsen's position (at this level of analysis) and remain not directly applicable only because the classist immoralist position is left incomplete, justificatory reasons for morality restrictions and selectivity are not given.

However, on closer look the position is not really a neat class-divided system, and it gets both more interesting and more problematic. As noted in the above quote, a classist immoralist can selectively extend his normally restricted moral concerns to outsiders he comes in contact with (such as a servant or mistress). The reason Nielsen gives for such an extension is simply that the classist immoralist "just happens to care for" the outsider.   But if people can be added for such a reason, why cannot people be dropped from moral status on the same grounds?   Dominant class members who have a bad case of body odor, or who are a little too efficient as business competitors, as well as people who do violent harm like rapists and arsonists, can very quickly become people for whom one no longer cares.

Nielsen writes that the classist immoralist "... has genuine moral relations with his own peers—the members of the elite class."[15] But apparently this is *not each* and *every* elite class member but *some* of these. For, in arguing how the classist immoralist can be a friend, and not be limited as an egoist to self-serving relationships, Nielsen states that "... the classist amoralist *can*, at least within his class, have such full-fledged relationships."[16]   Apparently, moral status *within* the elite class as well as extensions outside are not based on moral grounds "but on liking."

A test case for the classist immoralist is what to do about one's peers from the elite class who start to advocate publicly extending justice and "full-fledged relationships" to all or large numbers of the dominated class, instead of to just a select few? It seems to me that in this situation the classist immoralist would have to completely rethink her sparse, restricted moral theory unless, to avoid complications and problems, she simply slips into the purely egoistic immoralist program (but more on this option in a bit). Other questions arise: Does the classist immoralist withdraw friendship from these traitors to their peers? What happens when some elite class members' interests are sacrificed more severely for the good of the group? In general, how does one weigh acting on one's own interests versus the good of the class when conflicts arise?

Furthermore, once one opens the door to expanding or shrinking the moral group, according to whom one happens to care for, "class solidarity" is a fiction, a "purely class-based point of view" is no longer at issue. What one has then is a very strange moral account, in which each person's own personal morality appears to be based on relationships among a sliding group of people within and without one's social class, whose constituency at any given time is simply dependent upon whom one cares for at a given time, in a given circumstance. All others who fall outside the group at time t are treated to the "artful disguise of morality" to provide for their maximally efficient manipulation.

Nielsen writes that the classist immoralist may acknowledge that she is "morally arbitrary" in her judgments, but in asking the question, "Why should I be moral?" she is also asking as a corollary, "... why not be morally arbitrary, where my interests or the interests of my class are well served?"[17] As I have been suggesting, one answer to the question "Why not be morally arbitrary like the classist immoralist?" is simply—*for the sake of conceptual clarity,* to avoid much confusion about what the classist immoralist is really committed to and what morality is really about on this view.

Of course, one sure way that one can clear up much of the confusion is to understand and treat the *class aspect* of the classist immoralist's position as simply a transitional application of a purely egoistic position. The interests of one's class being well served becomes only an instrument for serving one's own personal interests; all the talk about treating one's class members as "friends" of moral solidarity is just more "artful disguise of morality" in order to further one's own interest.

This *enlightened* classist immoralist then, to use Pindar's analogy, may talk with the other foxes about their common interest in devouring the sheep (in other groups), yet this "greedy and crafty fox" will hide her purely egoistic program behind a second facade of illusory group loyalty. Such an agent then would work secretly behind this second facade, manipulating her fellow manipulators. In short, one way to clean up the confusion of the classist immoralist is to simply reduce the position to that of the personal egoist, a long-term calculating agent willing to select and restrain immorality through prohibitions, the development of habits and the use of "caring" relationships. And if this personal egoist clears away all elements of morality from the serious prescription category to the pile of manipulation tools, then she may be correctly said to be amoral.

Back to the "pre-enlightened" classist immoralist, Nielsen argues that the position is far more secure than his stunted version of individual egoism. I argue that this security point is vastly overrated. First of all, the classist immoralist as Nielsen describes her seems overly dependent on the social and political status quo and offers a normative model only for living in comfortable conditions as a result of good fortune.[18] Furthermore, as the foxes realize that their group membership from the new point of view of each fox can be adjusted up or down according to how each fox at a given time happens to care for whom, they at the same time are fully aware that companionship, comfort and recognition can suddenly change, and each fox remains vulnerable and uncomfortably dependent on the feelings of other foxes.

In this context, interesting *credibility problems* arise that may hinder the classist immoralist's ability to love and befriend, the alleged special advantage of this classist position. At any given time, is there not good reason for others of the same class to question whether the classist immoralist may decide to reduce those whom she befriends, not only from the larger de facto social class, but also from any current revised class to a still smaller revised group which may personally exclude them (perhaps she is even now manipulating them!)? On the other hand, how can the classist immoralist be confident that her assurances of inclusive friendship are not taken as disguised manipulations?

Consider the following hypothetical invitation by a classist immoralist. I suggest that it captures many of the problematic aspects of the position.

> Good evening, Bob. I know that you were not born into the fortunate economic, social and political position that I was, but I have enjoyed our acquaintance over the last several months, and I want to invite you to enter into a full-fledged friendship with me. I don't know if you are aware of this but I am a classist immoralist (I bet you're glad I'm no continually selfish egoist). As a classist immoralist, I can extend my moral concern to people like yourself or your family, who have been manipulated and used by me in the past for my own self-interest without concern for the consequences to your family. I know that you

are surprised by this opportunity from a member of the elite class. This extension of my moral favor, and your entrance into the moral domain, is not based on moral grounds but just because I, and I alone, happen to care for you at this time. If you agree to become my friend, and thereby attain moral status, then you can help me with my classy work and we can take advantage of people in your old neighborhood. Oh, as a sign of the genuine reciprocity of our relationship, I'll scratch your back if you scratch my back *and if* I happen to keep on caring for you.

Of course, if Bob does not follow Kant's suggestion and laugh in her face or shrink from her in disgust, he may be very puzzled with what he has here, and then attempt to ask the kinds of questions about moral theory, consistency, commitment to class, etc. that I have raised above. On the other hand, an observer may respond with complete puzzlement and be incredulous that such a person would be so honest with a new friend, incredulous that she would honestly lay out the whole (confusing) picture for Bob. But if a class immoralist cannot be honest in the activity of friendship-making, so emphasized by Nielsen, then maybe our class immoralist is really nothing more than a good old fashioned egoist blowing more smoke, albeit in some very strange patterns.

What is interesting about Nielsen's classist immoralist is that the concept does have some empirical applicability as a *descriptive* theory, in the sense that this kind of confused, unreflective, self-serving and uncourageous thinking may unfortunately be exactly how some people do think, function and carry out their lives. But in spite of its usefulness as some sort of descriptive model, as an ethical *prescriptive position* which can challenge morality as an *ideal* that is fitting for the intellectually talented, the courageous, and the efficient, classist immoralism cannot measure up to the task.

The amoral personal egoist position is in another league: it is a rather clean concept without the considerable theoretical difficulties that are intertwined throughout the description of the classist immoralist.

Notes

1   I owe this objection to my discussion of *personal* egoism to James Slinger of California State University at Fresno. Slinger's criticism in his commentary on my paper on egoistic reason-giving at the 1991 Pacific Division APA meeting was very helpful to me.

2   I here refer to what the amoral personal egoist holds as a normative position.
     In Chapter Seven I will clarify this further by also discussing in what sense
     her position is *not* a normative position and in what sense her position is *not*
     a theory, although it will have theoretical elements, after I discuss in what
     senses the amoral personal egoist does and does not justify her egoism.

3   Plato, *Republic*, trans. Grube-Reeve, p. 41 (365d).

4   Ibid., p. 36 (361b).

5   Except for 365d-366d, the question of being just or unjust is always discussed
     as a choice for an *individual* (for each person, for a man, for a young man,
     for someone, etc.). I understand Plato to be using the switch to first person
     plural here to emphasize that individual unjust persons (amoralists) can
     choose to take advantage of more intricate deceptions that one can pull off
     with the help of others in groups. After four paragraphs (by 366e) Plato
     returns again to discussion of a life of justice or injustice for the individual
     person.

6   Ibid., p. 41 (365c-d).

7   Ibid., p. 40 (365c).

8   Ibid., p. 41 (366c-d).

9   Nielsen, *Why Be Moral?*, pp. 290-91. Nielsen uses the terms "immoralist" and
     "amoralist" interchangeably, at some points in the chapter using one, in other
     spots using the other. I will use the "immoralist" term only in discussing
     Nielsen's account, primarily because I judge the classist immoralist position
     is confusing enough without adding that such an agent is also a selective
     and partial amoralist. I prefer to save the term "amoralist" for one who rejects
     morality and *all* its practices.

10   Another difference worth noting regards recognition of moral right and
     wrong. The amoral personal egoist as an amoralist recognizes morality and
     its specifics in the senses that she notices that people believe in it, that it
     consists in x,y, z etc., that it plays a certain role in most people's lives, that it
     has such and such consequences for individuals and society, etc.; but she
     does not recognize morality as valid for everyone, and specifically she does
     not recognize morality as validly applicable to her. On the other hand,
     Nielsen seems to suggest that the immoralist can know what is morally right
     in a stronger sense than just that she can recognize how it works in others'
     lives and how to use that for her own benefit. See p. 285 of *Why Be Moral?*

11   Ibid., p. 297.

[12] In the last chapter I discuss why the amoral personal egoist's program may be *systematically* self-defeating. Perhaps the egoist does ultimately shoot herself in the foot, but it is simplistic, naive and perhaps simply the product of wishful thinking to assume that the egoist's problems can be very easily explained in terms of the egoist's clumsy use of blunt and crude instruments.

[13] Ibid., pp. 295-96.

[14] Ibid., pp. 297-98.

[15] Ibid., p. 295.

[16] Ibid., p. 297. Emphasis is mine.

[17] Ibid., p. 298.

[18] Compare this comfy model for the elite with that of the amoral personal egoist, who is flexible enough to work efficiently in any class situation she finds herself and makes use of all opportunities, makes her own breaks if need be, through artistic deception and careful planning.

Part III

Edgar Egoist's Agency

Chapter Six

Edgar's "Ought" Language

In Part III, I offer further specification of the amoral personal egoist, with special emphasis on the unity of her thought and those features which make such an agency unique. In Chapter Six, I will focus on the egoist's use of normative language, including how this is the product both of the systematic unity of her thought and the special strategy required to move successfully in social traffic. In Chapter Seven, I will turn to what it means for the amoral personal egoist to have reasons for acting and to how she gives reasons to others. This discussion of Edgar's reasoning will complete my attempt to provide a basic, but still realistically detailed, account of the amoral egoist's distinct normative agency.

This further specification will describe a normative candidate that is neither a straw man like Nielsen's crude egoistic immoralist nor a meta-ethical bungler with a self-defeating practical program. The final product of these two chapters' discussions will be an account prepared with sufficient articulation so that a balanced and careful answer to "Why should I be moral?" can be properly addressed in Chapter Eight.

For reasons of brevity, I hereby call the disciplined and selective amoral personal egoist, which I have been describing, Edgar Egoist.[1] Hereafter, all references to what Edgar Egoist would say or do will be a convenient, short-handed way of talking about a normative agent who is an amoral personal egoist at the categorical level and as such is concerned with his long-term efficiency in maintaining this singular life-style.

My clarifying specification in these two chapters of Part III will have both positive and negative aspects. Its positive aspects will include describing and exhibiting those conceptual functions, linguistic tools, and social strategies in sufficient detail to prepare for the last chapter's discussion. However, part of the test of sufficient articulation is whether one's product of clarification has been efficiently distinguished from other possible or competing positions. Accordingly, an important part of my activity will focus on those key negative aspects: What Edgar Egoist's agency is not and need not be like, what Edgar does not and need not do, and what Edgar does not and need not say.

Some important challenges to the agency of Edgar Egoist fall under the category of consistency questions. In terms of the development of my concept of a viable and challenging Edgar Egoist, the consistency issue, and its many aspects, has been a catalyst in moving my specification of such an agent through many fruitful confrontations with what Edgar does not, and need not, do or say. Although I will not silence all consistency challenges to my concept of Edgar Egoist, I attempt to raise them to a different level, and apply them to a conceptually more intricate agent who thereby can function with more practical versatility. I have found that attempts in contemporary philosophic literature to write off the challenge of the amoral egoist on grounds of inconsistency have been premature; for the accounts of the amoral egoist which have been focused upon have been limited to less than strong and challenging candidates. While keeping in mind the reminder by J. A. Brunton that "The widespread detestation of Egoism ... is mainly a detestation of a way of life, not a complaint that the Egoist is lacking in sensitivity for linguistic discrimination ...,"[2] I make a strong attempt to develop a specification of Edgar Egoist's agency that is a sufficiently strong candidate, in the spirit of Plato's challenge, to which to bring the demands of consistency.

In this chapter, I discuss whether Edgar can be consistent in his use of normative language, but only after first specifying further some important conceptual and perceptual features of Edgar's agency. Edgar Egoist's illocutionary practices, I will argue, are best understood as practical developments of his being a unique kind of normative agent, conceiving himself as such, planning and establishing habits accordingly. Therefore, I will develop Edgar's linguistic and illocutionary practices with sufficient background before moving to their consistency evaluation.

I begin with a brief reminder of descriptive points from Chapter Two. Edgar holds, as his fundamental procedural principle, that he ought to pursue his own wants exclusively and disregard the wants and welfare of all others, unless the satisfaction of the want of another person is at the same time judged as a means of satisfying a priority want of Edgar's. In short, to Edgar Egoist, there is only one end and all other considerations are given instrumental value and relative importance.

Of course, consistent with this egoistic procedure and principle may be many kinds of wants and want priorities. An egoist may focus his practical life upon the pursuit of power, wealth, pleasures of the palate, aesthetic enjoyments, or philosophic reading. Also Edgar may radically change his interests over time and yet remain an egoist. He may give up poetry for pushpin, philosophic study for dice throwing, or drug pushing for politics. The key factor in judging whether he remains an egoist or has a "change of heart," and is no longer a true egoist, is whether or not the agent in question continues to evaluate all his transactions with other agents *exclusively* by the above single normative principle.

Furthermore, the egoist may seek to handle other persons either very crudely and blatantly selfishly or very cleverly with maximally concealed intentions, at least until the maximally productive payoff. In short, egoists may vary drastically both in the interests that they pursue and in the manner in which they attempt to handle other persons. But what is constant for every conceivable type of genuine egoist, including those that may die young and those that may be too timid to pursue their strongest desires, is that in every case the only normative principle that ultimately guides each and every prescription in interactions with others is the above fundamental procedural principle.

THE EGOIST'S *AGENT-ANSCHAUUNG*

To attend to the egoist's most fundamental procedural principle is an easy way to explain what it is to be an amoral personal egoist like Edgar, and how to distinguish this kind of agency from all others. But there is another aspect of being an egoist like Edgar, another feature of the concept which is essential in clarifying egoism and in distinguishing further between being an amoral personal egoist and being moral. This feature is that perceptual thread that runs through all of the egoist's normative transactional experience and unifies it over time as having a distinctive character. This perceptual feature is the egoist's perception of the normative status of all other persons, relative to himself. I call this unified perception or recognition over time of all other normative agents the egoist's *transactional experience unifying agent recognition* or, for short, the egoist's *agent-anschauung*.

I have used the terms "obstacles" and "resources" to refer to other people with whom Edgar Egoist must deal. Whether Edgar considers a person or group of persons as an obstacle or as a resource will depend upon such things as Edgar's confidence in his abilities, the nature of his wants *vis-a-vis* the wants of these others, and the suitability of others to be of service to him. In either case, the status of others in the eyes of Edgar is always in every transaction the same—something to be handled for one purpose only. This kind of perception of other persons in every transaction is a common thread to all Edgar Egoist's practical experience and it unites his successive and various transactions with separate people as a common effort to egoistically succeed. Edgar's *egoistic imperative*, "Treat all of humanity, except in my own person, always as a means only, and never as an end, as I treat myself," captures a single procedural principle, but it *also* reflects a distinctive perception and evaluation of human agents.

A complete picture of being an amoral personal egoist must then include both an account of the unique role of his fundamental procedural principle and an account of his *transactional experience unifying agent recognition* or his *agent-anschauung*. Both are essential elements of being an Edgar Egoist and recognizing oneself as such.

EDGAR'S "OUGHT" LANGUAGE AS A NATURAL DEVELOPMENT OF HIS AGENCY

Edgar's normative language in general, and his "ought" language in particular, can be best understood as a natural development of his being a practicing egoistic agent in society. To provide needed explanatory background to Edgar's unique use of "ought," I first turn to a point made by Karl Popper about a key scientific term. In his *Conjectures and Refutations: The Growth of Scientific Knowledge,* Popper relates how he once began a lecture to Vienna physics students with the following instructions:

> "Take pencil and paper; carefully observe, and write down what you have observed." They asked, of course, what I wanted them to observe. Clearly the instruction, "Observe!" is absurd .... Observation is always selective. It needs a chosen object, a definite task, an interest, a point of view, a problem.[3]

In beginning my discussion of Edgar's use of normative language, I take a cue from Popper's imaginative experiment. Consider without any background or contextual information the instruction, "Take pencil and paper; carefully write down what you ought to do." I suggest the bare instruction "Do what you ought to do" is also absurd, and not at all helpful, unless the instruction is contextually filled out.

The natural reply to such a bare instruction is "What ought I to do *about what?*" If one's audience were a class of students, like Popper's, the students might assume that the question was intended to elicit prudential rules of thumb about studying techniques; or they might assume that the subject matter of the class in question might be a key clue to the sort of prescriptions being requested. But if the teacher explicitly excluded beforehand such contextual hints or direction, then the students are back to square one, and then all the "... about what?" questions become very appropriate. Notice too, that if one gives a totally bare instruction, "Write down what you ought to do," without any subject matter limitations or contextual clues, then no consistent, "I ought to do ..." answer is any more or less appropriate, or any more or less to the point (what point?) than any other answer. One can provide one's own contextual criteria or point of view, as these student replies do: "I ought to use a lighter shade of lipstick" or "I ought not to eat so much bran cereal for breakfast."

For those students who do not care to "fire off" an "I ought to ..." with their own assumed end or point of view, their frustration will focus on trying to make sense out of the bare instruction. Such an incomplete, unspecified instruction is hard to handle because in everyday discourse prescriptive ends or points of view are either commonly assumed or clearly given by contextual clues. Sometimes ends are assigned by "ought"-statements, even if uttered totally out of context; for example, one's implied goal could be understood, even if uttered during a church service, from the "ought"-statement, "I ought to change my oil and filter." "Ought"-statements need an end, goal, or point of view, whether such is explicitly agreed to, contextually given, assigned by a single speaker, or simply assumed. The end or point of view suggests criteria in light of which the "ought"-statement can be seen as correct or necessary.

One such point of view that is often assumed by many people in serious practical matters, especially those that are clearly interpersonal, is the point of view of morality. The best definition of morality may be widely contested by philosophers, but considerable agreement persists that there is a concept (or a group of similar concepts) of morality that is in fact used by many philosophers and non-philosophers alike,[4] and that this concept is distinct from such concepts as prudence, law and custom. But this moral point of view is of course rejected by the amoral personal egoist; Edgar's normative end can be best understood by his egoistic imperative and his *agent-anschauung*. Therefore, Edgar's "ought"-statements and "right"-statements, expressing necessity and correctness, insofar as he is serious and not just playing with other people, will always be given in light of his singular egoistic goal. Any other goal or point of view, irrespective of context or deceptive claim or agreement, will never be assumed by an Edgar Egoist.

To help elucidate the key relationship between Edgar's special use of "ought" and "right"-statements and his exclusively egoistic point of view, I turn to the insight of Henry Sidgwick's discussion of the special meaning of *moral* judgments, as distinguished from prudential or legal judgments. Sidgwick asks,

> What definition can we give of 'ought,' 'right,' and other terms expressing the same fundamental notion? To this I should answer that the notion which these terms have in common is too elementary to admit of any formal definition ... . I find that the notion we have been examining, as it now exists in our thought, cannot be resolved into any more simple notions; it can only be made clearer by determining as precisely as possible its relation to other notions with which it is connected in ordinary thought, especially to those with which it is liable to be confounded.[5]

I agree with Sidgwick that terms like "ought" and "right" cannot be resolved into simpler definitive units. I also agree that the way to proceed in further clarification, in ordinary discourse as well as in philosophical distinction drawing, is to focus on other concepts with which these terms may be related and also with which they may be confused. An important amendment to Sidgwick's method for clarifying the uses of value terms such as "ought" and "right" is my suggestion to look for a key concept or *master concept* which may further specify the meaning of these terms in specific applications.

In the case of Edgar Egoist's serious uses of "ought" and "right," his uses are very different from those of us moralists. The egoist's master concept makes all the difference. Normal assumptions about specifying necessity or correctness in light of a common moral standard no longer apply. When Edgar makes serious "ought"-judgments, he understands himself (and if it were practicable, could convey his understanding to other persons) to be expressing a *necessity in light of the standard of being amorally egoistic*. Seriously prescribed "I ought to do X" statements amount simply to "I egoistically ought to do X" statements. Similarly, Edgar's serious "right"-statements he understands as expressing *correctness in light of his singular amorally egoistic goal*. In short, the unifying master concept of being an Edgar Egoist, as defined, specifies in a distinctive way all of Edgar's serious, fully prescriptive uses of "ought" and "right."

In light of the above, when discussing either what logically follows from Edgar Egoist's uses of "ought" or "right" or whether Edgar is consistent in such uses, one cannot just assume that Edgar's uses of "ought" constitute the same types of locution and illocution as the *apparently* similar locutions and illocutions of us non-egoists. Those similar master concepts which organize the normative thought of us moralists are dramatically absent from the conceptual unity of Edgar's thought, with its egoistic master concept identified by its egoistic imperative and unique *agent-anschauung*. Accordingly, I suggest that the amoral egoist's locutions and illocutions performed in making "ought"-statements will be of a distinct sort. Therefore, to accurately answer questions, about what follows from such egoistic "ought"-statements and with what these statements are consistent or inconsistent, one must be careful to attend to these illocutionary differences.

Furthermore, is it surprising, or not to be expected, that what follows from Edgar Egoist's "ought"-statements may not be consistent with what follows from similar "ought"-statements made by non-egoists? Are not questions of consistency about a position like Edgar's not questions about whether he is always consistent in action or language with non-egoists, but rather questions about whether Edgar's own position is consistent with itself: that is, whether in using normative language and in having and giving reasons Edgar can maintain a single consistent position over time. I will consider the following questions in evaluating Edgar's own consistency: (a) Must each and every one of Edgar's "ought"-statements be consistent with all others?; (b) can Edgar maintain a consistent program of using different kinds of "ought"-statements in first-, second- and third-person uses?; and (c) can Edgar maintain a single consistent program that involves different illocutionary acts when he refers to himself than when he refers to other agents?

THOUGHT EXPERIMENT: EDGAR AS NORMATIVE LANGUAGE INSTRUCTOR

To answer these consistency questions, as well as to provide further clarification of Edgar's use of normative language, including exhibiting the key role that the master concept of "being an egoist" plays in specifying Edgar's language choices, I offer the following thought experiment. Consider the comparison between two normative agents and their respective normative language practices. On the one hand, I will sketch the practical situation of a father, who is, I will assume, a morally serious person involved in teaching normative language to his child. With this paternal moral agent, I will compare and contrast the agency of Edgar Egoist, and the linguistic consequences of Edgar's applying his egoistic imperative in social traffic, and in particular in the tight social traffic of interaction with his son, Egbert. By seeing how Edgar must both instruct and carefully respond to his son, I will attempt to exhibit the complexity in Edgar's use of "ought"-language,[6] including the typical illocutionary differences between his first-, second-, and third-person "ought"-statements. With this fuller description of how an amoral personal egoist would wield "ought"-language in social traffic, I can then approach these questions of consistency with more promising results.

I begin my thought experiment with the morally serious father, call him Mike, who is teaching moral language to his daughter, Maureen, both through his own example and through his explicit direction. For simplicity, I take as this comparative moral agent a father who holds that there are genuine moral obligations one has a duty to perform; and that, among the many possible uses of normative language, one of its most important is to articulate for oneself and others what these obligations are and why they are such, and to help guide oneself and other agents, especially those for whom one has special responsibilities, to act in accord with these obligations. As his child becomes capable of interacting with others, Mike will react in many different ways to her in new situations as they occur. In different situations Maureen will elicit encouragement, prohibitions, laughter, praise, frowns, descriptions of silliness, and so forth, from her father. As Maureen's intellectual ability develops, Mike will conscientiously note for her what he considers the morally important or those situations in which one should carry out one's moral obligations.

Her father will take care to distinguish for Maureen, as soon as she is capable, between the different reasons in different situations for his encouragement and praise, for his disapproval and prohibitions, etc., especially noting why one kind of reason for his praise, or blame, applies in a given situation, when another kind of reason may not apply. Sometimes, this kind of father will encourage some alternative actions because the actions are morally right, emphasizing the criteria by which he is judging them to be right, and taking care to note that the moral character of the actions do not change merely because he or Maureen is involved, or because the action at issue is also in his interest, or in Maureen's interest, or in accord with the community wishes, or required by law. The context of moral decision-making, including such factors as whose interests are affected how, and the father's explanations of his reasons for his direction, prohibition, praise, etc., in specific situations, will convey, if he is reasonably consistent, the pattern that some "ought"-statements and "right"-statements are used by Mike in a very serious way, to capture rules of conduct that apply to all human agents, and are not presented as only in-house rules.

If Maureen is perceptive and learns well, she will watch carefully, not only her father's verbal direction for her guidance in tough situations, but also his use of moral language, his facial expressions, and his treatment of his own interests *vis-a-vis* those of others in those situations where he, the father, is the one in the tough practical spot. In short, Maureen will check whether and how her father treats moral obligations seriously and distinctly from other rules of conduct. Maureen will learn, if she is fortunate, whether and for what reason her father has all along treated her development in normative language use and reasoning as carefully initiating her into a common system of normative correctness in which she, her father, and all human beings are life-long members.

Of course, included in Mike's instruction, as well as in his daughter's questioning, will be those tough questions about which "ought"-statements express moral obligations for all moral agents, which express moral obligations for certain people in which situations, which express only prudential necessities, which express both moral and prudential guidelines in which situations, etc.

THE HANDLING OF A RESOURCE PERSON

I turn now to Edgar Egoist as normative language instructor, considering the situation in which his son Egbert's development has reached that stage at which Edgar can actively begin to guide his young resource person by initiating him in normative language use. It is important to emphasize up front that the practical matter of how to instruct Egbert is merely a specific application of the handling of a resource person, an imaginative application of the egoistic imperative. The important difference between handling Egbert and every other resource person is the frequency of transactions. Accordingly, Edgar will take special care to avoid the short-sighted sacrificing of the potential outcomes of future transactions that results from consistently making selfish normative judgments to bring about immediate results.

Related to the short-sightedness temptation is Edgar Egoist's maintenance of secrecy. In instructing Egbert in the use of normative language, Edgar, of course, will establish instruction patterns and rules for Egbert solely according to what is in the long-range best interests of *Edgar*, rejecting every other kind of nurturing principle or rationale as irrelevant to Edgar's fundamental normative principle. However, Edgar realizes that Egbert's maximal utility over time requires maintaining the secrecy of his (Edgar's) single egoistic principle and *agent-anschauung*. In short, both (a) Edgar's being an amoral personal egoist and (b) Edgar's need to conceal this fact from others are necessary in explaining Edgar's use of normative language in the audience of others, including his son, Egbert.

Therefore, in contrast to Mike Moralist, whose conscientious attempts to nurture his daughter Maureen include his initiating her into a common morality, in whose system of correctness father and daughter are participating members, Edgar Egoist's most fundamental normative principle excludes all others, including son Egbert, from its domain of application. Furthermore, efficient application of his egoistic principle requires that Edgar not share the principle, either in the sense of presenting it as a common principle or in the sense of sharing with any other person knowledge of Edgar's even holding the principle. So when Edgar initiates Egbert into a practice of using normative language in everyday situations, there are several ways he is *not* going about this normative instruction: when using "ought" and "right" in the presence of Egbert or when guiding Egbert's use of such terms, Edgar Egoist is *not* prescribing such judgments as necessary or correct within a system of correctness that applies to both him and Egbert, and which system of correctness he (Edgar) accepts as supremely authoritative; nor is Edgar Egoist about to reveal fully his egoistic character by just going about egoistically prescribing for himself alone and explicitly revealing this to his son, Egbert, and then letting the chips fall as they may. The latter approach would soon become self-defeating as his son Egbert's abilities as an agent develop. Secondly, if Edgar took this latter approach he would fail to develop the "social" potential of egoism by neglecting to fully utilize the human resources at his disposal. It is the opportunistic, and necessarily more deceitful, development of egoism that Edgar presents rather than the anti-social, easily recognizable form.

The exact nature of those rules of conduct for son Egbert, which rules Edgar judges will be most egoistically efficient for himself (Edgar), will largely depend upon Edgar's estimation of such factors as the kind of community in which they reside, the kind of peer influence which Egbert will experience, Egbert's intelligence and capacity for independent thought, Edgar's own ability to play the major influential role in Egbert's normative development, etc. However, regardless of the particular content of these rules for Egbert, the reason for Edgar's guidance of Egbert's use of such language is always procedurally the same: what is egoistically efficient for Edgar.

If Edgar finds himself in an "instruction situation" with Egbert, in which the pattern of conduct that Edgar has been encouraging for Egbert conflicts with what Edgar *prima facie* prescribes for himself, with Edgar's decision and example on the line, then Edgar will have to weigh (a) the probable damage to the normative pattern that has been encouraged for Egbert, including the probable success of trying to patch up his (Edgar's) model and its role in establishing that pattern for Egbert versus (b) the probable egoistic gain accrued from acting on the *prima facie* egoistic prescription. Of course, the procedure for deciding these difficult and very complicated matters is again simply to apply the fundamental egoistic principle. If the gain is great enough relative to his current and long-range wants, Edgar may be willing to gamble on his verbal dexterity and acting ability to minimize model and pattern damage through pleas of confusion, emotion, weakness of will, etc., whatever it takes to get the job done.

For example, Edgar may be encouraging and instructing Egbert to avoid the path of chemical dependency, in particular the habit of illegal drug use. At the same time, Edgar may find that he can, through his business, involve himself in the very lucrative marketing and network distribution of such illegal drugs. Edgar will have to weigh the risks, both legal and personal, especially the risks of possibly damaging his credibility and guidance role with Egbert. Of course, whether Edgar takes such risks and how he makes judgments based on his egoistic imperative will largely depend on what Edgar wants most. If Edgar believes that the huge drug distribution profit can provide him with those activities and things that he wants most, he may even risk the derailing of his normative program for Egbert, perhaps even risk the life of Egbert himself. By contrast, Mike Moralist would rule out on principle any activity or example that could harm seriously the morality or welfare of his daughter Maureen. Maureen's own moral development and welfare are built into Mike's basic normative program. But with Edgar, Egbert's instrumental value as a resource person is totally relative to Edgar's want priorities and his estimation of efficiency questions over time.

Now it may be objected that an egoist such as Edgar would never be a father and, hence the illustrative merits of the father comparisons are lost. I reply that, first of all, there is no inconsistency in an egoist's being a biological father and spending time with his son.[7] The decision to be a father for the egoist is by definition a matter of egoistic strategy, like everything else; of course, for an egoist to so choose would require certain wants and long-range goals that many egoists would not pursue. But, in any case, the illustrative purpose of comparing these two fathers is twofold: (a) to emphasize the conceptual priority of the master concept of being an egoist to the egoist's illocutionary use of normative language; and (b) to exhibit Edgar's illocutionary purposes in prescribing for himself versus communicating with others. These same conceptual and illustrative points could be made using the example of Edgar Egoist "handling" the paper boy-turned-investigative-reporter, who stays in close contact with the fascinating Edgar. The special advantage of illustrating this major concept-illocutionary-use relationship with the father-instructing-child situation is that it emphasizes how early the master concepts of being an egoist and being moral can come into play in initiating a child into normative practice.

EDGAR'S MULTIPLE "OUGHT"-USES.

I turn now to a brief analysis of Edgar's first-person "ought"-statements, his second-person "ought"-statements to his son Egbert, as well as third-person "ought"-statements about other people in the presence of his son Egbert. If my analysis of Edgar's normative communication with, and in front of, Egbert is descriptively correct, the analysis will also be largely accurate about how Edgar uses "ought"-language with all other persons, since Egbert's normative status, based upon Edgar's egoistic principle, is no different than any other normative agent's—they are all egoistic resources for Edgar.

Conceptually organizing and appraising his practical world under the egoistic master concept, Edgar Egoist only seriously prescribes and endorses those value judgments in which he is both the maker of the value judgments and at the same time the subject of the judgment, for example: "I ought to do x," "Edgar Egoist ought to do x." When speaking to or about any other person, Edgar is never seriously prescribing for others, in the sense of seriously offering guidance in a common normative system, as Mike Moralist does when he offers guidance to daughter Maureen with "ought"- and "right"-statements. The domain of Edgar's serious "ought" guidance is limited to only one agent.

At this point two related questions arise in light of the unique limitations in Edgar's serious use of egoistic "ought"-statements. One question has to do with consistency and whether Edgar Egoist can remain consistent in social traffic. The second related question is whether, in order to avoid entangling himself in inconsistency, Edgar must avoid all communication with other people using normative language. If this second question can only be answered in the affirmative, two theoretic disadvantages accrue to Edgar's egoistic position. One disadvantage is that Edgar's amorally egoistic position becomes thereby socially isolated and therefore is less appealing as a normative option. A second disadvantage is that, if all value-language communication with others is terminated, Edgar's secretive and deceptive approach to others may become suspect and, therefore, Edgar's language strategy would be self-defeating and inefficient given his egoistic imperative. My subsequent discussion of both consistency and the related question about to what extent Edgar's agency is a truncated, less interesting agency will result in a more sophisticated account of Edgar's position by clarifying the conceptual organization and social tactics behind Edgar's unique use of normative language.

In speaking with his son Egbert, Edgar can use second-person "ought"-statements of the form "You ought to to x" in two different ways, both of which allow him value-language communication with Egbert without involving Edgar in genuine inconsistency. One way that Edgar guides Egbert in the second person is with technical means-ends "ought"-statements of the form, "If you want X, you ought to do Y." Sometimes the antecedent is explicitly stated, for example, "If you want to develop a healthy body, you ought to eat a sufficient amount of fruits and vegetables." At other times the antecedent may be contextually assumed or implied: for example, Edgar saying on the steps, "Egbert, you ought to tie your shoe laces," with contextually assumed antecedent, "If you do not want to break your neck."

However, the second kind of second-person "ought"-use by which Edgar guides Egbert's actions and "nurtures" Egbert's normative development is by far the more interesting use, insofar as this sort of "ought"-use involves deceptively concealing a special antecedent in accord with carefully planned egoistic procedure. This use of "ought" conceals the following procedural antecedent, "If you (Egbert or any other person) are to bring about your most efficient utility as a resource person for my (Edgar's) egoistic agency, (then) ... ." Edgar then can follow this antecedent, which is spoken only to himself, with any "ought"-statement he wants that would be helpful in social traffic. Of course, consistent with his maintenance of secrecy policy, Edgar always keeps this standard antecedent secretly to himself, saying it silently to himself as a reservation for, and giving meaning to, the uniquely deceptive guidance for Egbert.

In summary, Edgar Egoist's second-person "ought"-statements to Egbert (or any other person) are never seriously prescribed as correct guidance within a common normative system of interacting agents. Edgar's second-person "ought"-uses, while providing both communication with and guidance of others, consist in each case of a consequent in a hypothetical "if-ought" statement that functions in a way entirely distinct from Edgar's first-person uses that are seriously prescribed as applications of Edgar's fundamental normative principle. These second- and third-person consequents are either of two kinds: the second halves of technical, means-end, "If-ought" statements or the self-serving guides for others whose hypothetical antecedents consist of procedurally concealed antecedents that reflect the purely egoistic wishes of Edgar Egoist.

Similarly, in the witness of Egbert, Edgar can go beyond the restrictions of his serious prescriptions required by his fundamental egoistic principle, and communicate with, and provide a self-serving guidance for, others *in the third person*. Again, Edgar may make hypothetical "if-ought" efficiency statements expressing a hypothetical necessity between the possible wants of others and the suggested means expressed by "ought": as "If those parents want to eliminate drugs in the school, then they ought to actively support every drug awareness and discipline program which the schools initiate." Or Edgar Egoist can communicate with, and provide a self-serving guidance for others by deceitfully concealing the antecedent of a hypothetical "If-ought" statement such as, "If Egbert and his friends are to become the most useful resource persons for my long-range egoistic purposes, then they ought to develop the discipline to maintain healthy, drug-free bodies."[8]

Given this value-language communication program, is Edgar consistent? I suggest this program can be consistently applied. The test case, of course, is the situation in which Edgar judges that he *egoistically ought* to do X while at the same time offering to Egbert a deceptively delivered "If-ought" hypothetical that suggests Egbert ought *not* to do X. In such a case, an action is apparently advised both to be done and not to be done by apparently similar agents. For example, Edgar judges at time t that he egoistically ought to begin (or continue) to distribute illegal drugs. At the same time Edgar may deceptively communicate guidance to Egbert that he, Egbert, ought never to use, buy, or sell illegal drugs; of course, the concealed antecedent to the "ought" guidance for Egbert is Edgar Egoist's standard, "If he, Egbert, is to become the most useful resource person for Edgar, (then) ... ."

Why this unusual linguistic program can be consistently applied, and why Edgar need not be inconsistent in his use of "ought" comes down to the fact that Edgar is using different kinds of "ought"-statements, performing entirely different illocutionary acts in first-person versus his second- and third-person "ought"-statements. These different "ought"-uses and different illocutionary acts are a result of Edgar's unique master concept that leaves no room in Edgar's practical program for a common normative truth-discerning practice, nor a single, and commonly applied, "ought"-use that guides all persons in the same objective fashion. In short, Edgar is not saying and doing the same thing in first versus second- and third-person "ought"-use. In serious first-person uses, Edgar is guiding himself alone by reason of egoistic necessity relationships, given his master concept and practical programs, including linguistic ones. In second and third-person uses, Edgar is never seriously setting normative-guidance requirements in a *common* program, for himself *and* others. Rather Edgar is often attempting to manipulate others by reason of deceptively used hypotheticals, as a tactical maneuver for exclusively egoistic ends.

THE STRANGE-USE OBJECTION

In order to further clarify these important locutionary and illocutionary differences, as well as the conceptual and developmental source of these differences, I consider two objections to Edgar's "ought"-use program: (1) that Edgar's uses of "ought" are strange uses, and (2) that Edgar's program cannot account for universalizability, as a feature of linguistic terms or as a feature of giving reasons.

First is the strangeness objection, that Edgar's linguistic practice with its multi-purpose, gear-switching "ought"-statements is very strange. J. A. Brunton's reply to this objection is right on the mark:

> If we are just to say to the Egoist that he is using words in a queer kind of way, he is likely to retort that he can find no other words to suit his purpose as well. Words like 'want' and 'desire' will certainly not replace 'ought' since the Egoist must somehow distinguish between his settled policy of life and his momentary whims.[9]

And an amoral personal egoist like Edgar has a conceptually and practically sophisticated policy of life and a proportionately sophisticated normative language system. When Edgar is first developing strategy in applying his egoistic imperative, it may be helpful for him to avoid confusion by using the term "should" instead of "ought" in second- and third-person communication in social traffic. But as Edgar gets more proficient in distinguishing, and not confusing, in his thought the egoistic and hypothetical uses, he will likely discontinue this practice, in the event that this pattern may be recognized and draw curious attention to his conceptual and normative reasons for his linguistic preferences. In short, Edgar will decide that this "ought-should" combination is not deceptive enough, and go with the same term "ought" with its different uses.

In agreeing with Brunton's point that the use of "ought" serves Edgar's purposes very well, I suggest further that Edgar's multiple "ought"-uses look queer only in isolation and out of context. These "ought"-uses become most understandable only if Edgar's master concept and egoistic imperative are clearly understood, as well as his tactical judgments in social traffic. Of course, Edgar knows that he will be most efficient if others, including his son, Egbert, do not fully understand his multiple uses of "ought" and his distinct illocutionary acts. For to understand fully his language and linguistic intentions is to understand his master concept and his strategy, and thereby to be in a position to frustrate his plans. Conceptual differences make possible an "ought"-use program that can be used consistently; Edgar's egoistic strategy takes advantage of these conceptual differences to conceal the full meaning of and distinction between his multiple "ought"-uses.

To expand my discussion on these points, let us consider what is involved if Egbert catches his father Edgar in an apparent inconsistency. Of course, Edgar, as well as Mike Moralist, can misspeak or slip up in a careless or absentminded fashion. But I consider the situation in which Edgar knows what he is doing, is carefully applying his egoistic imperative and his linguistic program for communication with others. In such a situation, Edgar has several options when confronted by Egbert with an apparent inconsistency. First of all, he can try to bluff his way through the predicament, by claiming that he was not aware of some facts of the situation, or that he misspoke and that he meant to say B instead of A, or that he is not his normal, effective self for some physical or psychological health reason. The second option for Edgar is to take another shot at concealing or covering up his second- or third-person "ought"-use by referring to a hypothetical "If, ought" statement or referring to some rule or principle of conventional morality. The third option is for Edgar to defend his consistency by explaining *fully* each of the "ought"-uses at issue, thereby unveiling his specific strategy, but also unveiling his egoistic agency and all that such an agency involves.

Consistent with his maintenance of secrecy policy, Edgar would avoid option three at all costs. Edgar knows enough about other people to know that he is better off in social traffic to be caught as an imperfect logician than revealed as a full-fledged amoral egoist. Edgar may agree with Brunton about the valuation people give to egoistic partiality versus logical error: "The widespread detestation of Egoism ... is mainly a detestation of a way of life, not a complaint that the egoist is lacking in sensitivity for linguistic discrimi-nation."[10] In short, when son Egbert catches his father Edgar in an apparent inconsistency, the major problem beneath the surface is not a logical one, but one of substantive normative principle. The major problem is not consistency but deceit. Brunton continues,

> ... if we are not to confuse matters of substance with matters of linguistic analysis, then ... our linguistic analysis must make allowance for these matters of substance and not strangle them at birth.[11]

My description of Edgar Egoist's multiple "ought"-uses, with its concealed accounts of genuine egoism on the one hand, and the deceitful uses of "If-ought" hypotheticals on the other, attempts to capture how an amoral personal egoist would maintain a consistent, linguistic program in social traffic, while not needlessly distracting nor diminishing the unique, normative differences of such an agent.

OBJECTION TWO: CAN EDGAR ACCOUNT FOR UNIVERSALIZABILITY?

I turn now to the second objection, that Edgar Egoist cannot account for universalizability. Universalizability is that set of related issues about whether normative language and normative judgments entail universal principles, and what role these relationships should play in ethics. Universalizability has been approached in at least the following two ways: (1) as a characteristic of evaluative terms, shared also by non-evaluative terms, by virtue of each term's rules for application; and (2) as a characteristic of the logic of moral reasoning, a logical consequence of the practice of giving reasons for one's evaluative judgments or, put differently, a consequence of the distinctive role that "because" plays in argumentative discourse. The essential claim of the universalizability thesis in any of its related versions is that an appeal to reasons, whether for applying evaluative terms or in support of particular evaluative judgments, entails or logically commits one to the acceptance of universal rules—in the case of terms to their rules of application, in the case of judgments to universal evaluative principles. From each of these two approaches to universalizability one can develop a related, but distinct, argument that attempts to show the amoral personal egoist to be inconsistent. The question that I will consider is whether Edgar Egoist's use of evaluative terms like "ought" or his use of "ought"-judgments imply his acceptance of a universal principle that is inconsistent with being an amoral personal egoist.

In his book *Freedom and Reason,*[12] R. M. Hare primarily approaches universalizability as a feature of evaluative words. Although Hare discusses the universalizability of normative judgments, in terms of space and emphasis the "logic of 'ought' " gets top billing over the logic of reason-giving. I look to Hare's fruitful discussion for several distinct senses of universalizability, which can be then applied as a check on Edgar Egoist's consistency in language and program.

According to Hare, universalizability along with prescriptivity together comprise "... the logical framework provided by the word 'ought' ... ."[13] This logical framework is a necessary ingredient of moral argument, according to Hare, along with (1) the facts of the situation, (2) inclinations or wants of the people concerned, and (3) an imagination to consider oneself in the situation of others.[14] In explaining this theory of moral reasoning, Hare discusses how these ingredients are used to reject or falsify a practically possible "ought"-judgment.

> Just as science, seriously pursued, is the search for hypotheses and the testing of them by the attempt to falsify their particular consequences, so morals, as a serious endeavour, consists in the search for principles and the testing of them against particular cases. Any rational activity has its discipline, and this is the discipline of moral thought: to test the moral principles that suggest themselves to us by following out their consequences and seeing whether we can accept *them.*

> ... Because moral judgements have to be universalizable, B cannot say that he ought to put A into prison for debt without committing himself to the view that C, who is *ex hypothesi* in the same position *vis-a-vis* himself, ought to put *him* into prison; and because moral judgements are prescriptive, this would be, in effect, prescribing to C to put him into prison; and this he is unwilling to do, since he has a strong inclination not to go to prison.[15]

Of course, Edgar Egoist would never seriously participate in moral reasoning so defined. He may carefully study the facts of a situation, including the inclinations of all parties. And, as part of his attempt to attain a better understanding of his resources and the consequences of possible actions, Edgar might imagine what it would be like if he were in a situation with such and such consequences. But this latter thought experiment would have no direct role in his egoistic thinking. The only reason for Edgar to reject an "ought"- judgment is on an egoistic basis; the only first-person, seriously-prescribed "ought"-judgments are egoistic "oughts," with no implied prescription for others.

In turning to universalizability itself, Hare states:

> Offences against the thesis of universalizability are logical, not moral. If a person says "I ought to act in a certain way, but nobody else ought to act in that way in relevantly similar circumstances," then, on my thesis, he is abusing the word 'ought'; he is implicitly contradicting himself.[16]

Rather than describing his "ought"-uses as abuse, Edgar would prefer to describe them as imaginative and enterprisingly novel uses. And, as discussed above, Edgar's "ought"-statements about other people are simply different than any of his serious first-person egoistic "ought"-statements. What is said and what is done in saying it are different in the two cases. Edgar is simply not affirming both A and not-A. J. A. Brunton has labeled the assymmetry in the egoist's attitude towards himself and towards others as the egoist's "double-think." Brunton argues that, "... the entertaining of an 'ought' under a hypothesis does not have the weight of an obligation, an 'ought' categorically accepted as a principle." Brunton uses a chess example and a war example to illustrate his point; the latter example is the following:

> ... one cannot be using "ought" in quite the same way, or with the same breath, if, as an army commander, one says of the opposing general, "he 'ought' never to have attacked us on the left flank" *and* "He did just as he ought, attacking us on the left flank. He's won the battle for us." In these examples we are *contrasting* the sense of

"ought" which relates to a hypothesis (if he knows his game, "chess" or "war") and that which relates to the general desires of the egoist. Putting the matter in general terms; since, in a competitive game one wants one's opponent to lose, any putting oneself in his place, taking his point of view, will be subordinated to the desire that he make the *wrong* moves, that he ought to do from the Egoist's point of view what he ought not to do from his own.[17]

Brunton goes on to argue that any contradiction here is only apparent rather than genuine.

The "double-think" involved in my chess, and, perhaps more clearly, army commander examples, only appears to involve an incomprehensible contradiction ("He ought to move the knight—He ought to be stopped from moving the knight") ("He ought not to have attacked on the left—He did just as he ought, attacking on the left"), if the adoption by an individual of two points of view and his playing one off against the other is a phenomenon which is difficult to understand. And this is far from being the case.[18]

In Brunton's terminology, my account of Edgar Egoist's multiple "ought"-uses involves a "triple-think" phenomenon that also is not difficult to understand, but is essential for understanding how an amoral egoist like Edgar would move in social traffic. In addition to the "double-think" "ought"-uses involving efficiency hypotheticals, Edgar uses deceptive, manipulative "if-ought" statements with concealed antecedents referring to his egoistic goals. At this "triple-think" level, using Brunton's analogy, Edgar functions in social traffic like an army commander, who, through the use of intelligence forces, seeks to provide propaganda or advice to the opposing general that is calculated to be (but not to be disclosed as such) to the benefit of and in accord with the plans of the deceptive commander.

I move now to a closer look at Hare's account of universalizability and to questions regarding in what sense Edgar's "ought"-statements are universalizable and in what sense they are not. Hare's account in *Freedom and Reason* suffers from the confusion of using "using 'ought' universalizably" in two distinct ways without distinguishing them. The stronger version appears in his discussion of moral reasoning and the process of evaluating alternative "ought"-judgments.

(U1) When we are trying, in a concrete case, to decide what we ought to do, ... (we are looking for) ... an action ... which we are at the same time prepared to accept as exemplifying a principle of action to be

prescribed for others in like circumstances (universalizability). If ... we
find that, when universalized, it yields prescriptions which we cannot
accept, we reject this action as a solution to our moral problem—if we
cannot universalize the prescription, it cannot become an "ought."[19]

Now it is certainly not surprising that Edgar's use of "ought" is
not universalizable in this sense of (U1), for (U1) is not an ethically
neutral consistency principle but rather functions in Hare's theory
of moral reasoning as a principle of impartiality,[20] which is very
different from Edgar's egoistically prescriptive uses of "ought." So
one argument against Edgar based on Hare's universalizability (U1)
of "ought" as a special evaluative word comes to this: the egoist is
contradicting himself because he is using the word "ought" in a way
which fails to prescribe impartially between himself and others.
But this argument, which may be effective against many value-
language users, leaves Edgar unscathed. His logic of "ought" is
meant to be different from the most prevalent or ordinary logic of
the term. Edgar's failure as judged by the standard of (U1) amounts
not to a violation of consistency but a disinterest in linguistic
conformity, which is easily explicable in terms of Edgar's master
concept and egoistic imperative.

Although understandable and common for us non-egoists, it is
nevertheless presumptuous and mistaken to say that Edgar Egoist is
contradicting himself, when he utters several statements each
containing "ought," in such combination that, *if* these utterances
were prescribed by an advocate of (U1), this (U1) "ought"-user
would be contradicting himself. The presumption and mistake
here would be similar to the presumption and error of Edgar
Egoist, if he (totally out of character) shouted "Inconsistency!
Inconsistency!" from the back of church each time the minister
repeated that every person ought to act unselfishly with regard to
his fellow man. If Edgar presumed that the minister is implying
that he, Edgar, *egoistically ought* to act non-egoistically, then Edgar
would take the statement as an inconsistency. Similarly, if one
naturally assumed that Edgar's different uses of "ought," whether
about himself or others, were all a single, serious and honest use of
a term that commonly applies to others in the same fashion, then
of course one mistakenly takes his utterances to be an inconsistent
use of the same term, rather than a consistently applied program
with multiple and diverse uses of the same term.

Turning now to Hare's second way of discussing "using 'ought' universalizably," Hare discusses universalizability also as a characteristic of evaluative judgments, in virtue of the logic of giving reasons in their support:

(U2): ... by calling a judgment universalizable I mean only that it logically commits the speaker to making a similar judgment about any thing which is either exactly like the subject of the original judgment or like it in the relevant respects. The relevant respects are those which formed the grounds of the original judgment.[21]

Note that universalizability so defined is no longer a special feature of the one word "ought," but is a feature of judgments in general, whether they be "ought"-judgments, "good"-judgments, or non-evaluative judgments. Universalizability in the sense of (U2) is truly a logical thesis in the sense that, as D. H. Monro puts it, it merely demands "... consistency in the use of language as a means of communication,"[22] and does not demand further that one's grounds for the universalizable judgment must be such that the use of the crucial terms be conformable with the most prevalent or morally appropriate uses.

It is no doubt (U2) which Hare has in mind in Chapter I when he says that,

... the feature of value-judgments which I call universalizability is simply that which they share with descriptive meaning ... . If I call a thing red, I am committed to calling anything else like it red. And if I call a thing a good X, I am committed to calling any X like it good.[23]

In accord with (U2), if I say that I ought to do W on the grounds that I have properties A, B, and C and that the situation has features X, Y, and Z, then I am committed to admitting that all similar persons, in having properties A, B, and C, in similar situations, having features X, Y, and Z, ought to do W as well. It is the logic of giving reasons for any (and all) "ought"-judgments, whether the speaker's grounds for so using "ought" are representative of typical or bizarre uses of the term, that universalizability *qua* (U2) is required on grounds of consistency. Note that the difference between (U1) and (U2) is not merely a difference in emphasis, the former emphasizing the universalizability of terms and the latter of judgments. For (U2) can be restated with its emphasis on terms rather than judgments, as follows:

(U3): To say a term (whether evaluative or not) is used universalizably is to say that the speaker is logically committed to using that term with respect to other persons and in other situations which are similar in the relevant respects, the relevant respects being the speaker's original grounds for so using the term.

To evaluate how Edgar's position stacks up against the consistency standards of (U2) and (U3), I attend to the following two judgments by Edgar:

A) I, Edgar Egoist, ought to distribute illegal drugs.

B) My son Egbert ought to distribute illegal drugs.

Edgar may seriously prescribe A as egoistically necessary: whether he does or does not so prescribe A in a given situation will depend upon whether or not Edgar believes acting on A would be a correct application of his egoistic imperative. Let us assume in a given situation that Edgar does so seriously prescribe A. If (U2) and (U3) merely demand consistency in language use, to remain consistent, must Edgar also seriously prescribe B, whose subject, Egbert, is similar in many respects to Edgar (same family, same curly hair, etc.)? I argue that Edgar can consistently refrain from prescribing B and successfully meet the demands of (U2) and (U3), because, as the amoral personal egoist that he is, Edgar builds into the "relevant respects" of his original grounds, for all his serious normative judgments, the procedural limitations and exclusive partiality that are uniquely that of the personal amoral egoist, as I have characterized him.

First of all, as I have discussed, Edgar categorically prescribes for himself alone, such being the limited reach of his fundamental normative principle. The question of whether the logic of (U2) and (U3) require Edgar to prescribe for others *in the same way* turns on the freedom of the maker (speaker) of the judgment to define the "relevant respects" of person and situational similarity into the original grounds for making the judgment or using the normative term. When Edgar categorically precribes A, included in the original grounds for A are: (a) that he is an amoral personal egoist whose normative guidance is specified for one person only, and (b) that it is he, Edgar, who is the subject of judgment A. To categorically prescribe A is for Edgar to egoistically prescribe A; and two key and fundamental reasons for making and seriously prescribing that kind of judgment are (a) and (b). Edgar Egoist meets the logical requirements of (U2) and (U3), as long as he continues to make similar "ought"-judgments about relevantly similar persons in relevantly similar situations. Based on his original grounds, to make a serious, categorical judgment like B is to make an "ought"-judgment in a changed situation about a relevantly dissimilar person: such a judgment Edgar need not make on logical grounds alone.

Now what makes a character like Edgar both a genuine egoist and thoroughly consistent is that he builds into the original ground for any of his serious, categorical "ought"-judgments those "relevant respects" which distinguish Edgar Egoist's prescribing from all other value-judgments. This egoistically defined system of prescription is designed expressly *not to extend* this favored position *to the universal class of all human beings*. But the designed neglect in extending the special favored position of subject-prescribing to the universal class of human beings is distinct from any alleged neglect on his part in *consistently applying his egoistic discrimination universalizably*: "The hell with others in any case!"

To summarize this second objection based on universalizability, I have argued that Edgar Egoist can consistently use "ought"-language in an intelligible way, in spite of the fact that such language uses may appear bizarre to the non-egoist. The fruitful discussion of R. M. Hare has helped clarify two distinct interpretations of universalizability. Under one interpretation (U2 and U3), merely principles requiring consistency in language, Edgar can meet the demand for universalizability. But under an ethically non-neutral interpretation (U1), not surprisingly Edgar Egoist fails to measure up to a principle of impartiality.

In this chapter I have presented a descriptive account of how an amoral personal egoist, like Edgar, can use "ought" language in an intelligible way that can avoid contradiction. I have presented a linguistic program for Edgar Egoist that is both (a) efficient and not self-defeating and (b) capable of being consistently applied, with sufficient discipline and practice. The key to both the program's efficiency and its potential for consistent application lies in its novel multiple "ought"-use system in which Edgar Egoist performs different illocutionary acts in using "oughts" in different ways with himself and others. Through the use of both hypothetical "If-ought" statements and concealed antecedents in deceptively manipulative "If-ought" statements, Edgar can consistently talk to others about "what they ought to do," without retreating one iota from his serious fundamental normative commitment to *exclusively* self-referring, *egoistic* "oughts."

Notes

1   My choice of the name Edgar was made many years ago, during early drafts of this book, and since then the name seems to work in a number of respects, including that no one named Edgar has yet objected to it. Recently a commentator has suggested the name Egor, perhaps as more descriptively appropriate. But as I have worked hard to show, the amoral personal egoist need not be a beast without intelligent and long-range planning, need not be a brute who lives alone. The strongest-case analysis, I suggest, is a highly social even unassuming Edgar, not an Egor on the rampage.

2   J. A. Brunton, "Egoism and Morality," *The Philosophical Quarterly*, vol. 6 (1956), reprinted in Joseph Margolis, ed., *Contemporary Ethical Theory* (New York: Random House, 1966), p. 295.

3   Karl R. Popper, *Conjectures and Refutations: The Growth of Scientific Knowledge* (New York: Harper & Row, 1965), p. 46.

4   For an interesting account of the status of this concept of morality, see Elizabeth Anscombe's "Modern Moral Philosophy" in Thomson, Judith J. and Dworkin, Gerald, eds., *Ethics* (New York: Harper & Row, 1968), pp. 186-210. Anscombe argues that using "ought" or "right" in a specific moral sense as "is obliged" or "is bound" or "is required" is to participate in a mistaken practice of perpetuating the unintelligible use of these terms, continuing to foster the survival of a concept "... outside the framework of thought that made it a really intelligible one" (p. 193). Anscombe argues that this special moral sense of "ought" and "right" is a direct descendant of the concepts of being bound or permitted *within* a law conception of ethics; that this formerly dominant concept of a law conception of morality has been "given up"; and, therefore, that its concepts of being bound or required have "lost their root." Hence, claims Anscombe, the descendant, special moral uses of "ought" and "right" also float adrift, untethered to an intelligible conceptual framework.

5   Sidgwick, *Methods of Ethics*, pp. 32-33.

6   My discussion below on normative language will attend to Edgar's "ought"-language uses, but similar points and distinctions can also be made by focusing on Edgar's use of "right," "wrong," etc. For reasons of brevity I do not attempt to provide a complete system of all egoistic normative language use. Rather I provide a model with "ought"-uses and I emphasize the relationship between these uses and the conceptual features and strategy which explain them.

7 Of course, the quality of time spent with his son is another matter. This very interesting question is very much related to Chapter Eight's discussion regarding whether Edgar Egoist can be a genuine friend to another person, including his son.

8 A key premise here is that drug-free resource persons are more reliable and more efficient persons, and therefore are more useful to Edgar's program and its efficient application.

9 J. A. Brunton, "Egoism and Morality," in Margolis, *Contemporary Ethical Theory*, p. 294.

10 Ibid., p. 295.

11 Ibid. See also Iris Murdoch in "Vision and Choice in Morality," in *Proceedings of the Aristotelian Society*, supp. vol. 30 (1956): 32-58. Murdoch advises the reader to return frequently to the phenomena, in this case to my hypothetical delineation of egoism (Murdoch's topic was morality), so that the philosophical technique or methodology used to describe egoism (For Murdoch: morality) is accounting for all the phenomena and not just a select group.

12 R. M. Hare, *Freedom and Reason* (New York: Oxford University Press, 1965).

13 Ibid., p. 92.

14 According to Hare this imaginative ingredient includes a readiness to be imaginative in a certain way: "All that is essential to it is that B should disregard the fact that he plays the particular role in the situation which he does, without disregarding the inclinations which people have in situations of this sort. In other words, he must be prepared to give weight to A's inclinations and interests as if they were his own. This is what turns selfish prudential reasoning into moral reasoning" (p. 94). Of course, for Edgar to develop this sort of imagination is simply on his view egoistically inefficient.

15 Ibid., p. 92.

16 Ibid., p. 32.

17 J. A. Brunton, "The Devil Is Not a Fool or Egoism Re-Visited," *American Philosophical Quarterly* 12 (October 1975): 324.

18 Ibid., p. 325.

19 Hare, *Freedom and Reason*, pp. 89-90.

[20] In his lucid discussion of universalizability, D. H. Monro uses this distinction between a logical principle of consistency and a moral principle of impartiality in criticizing Hare.   He correctly adds that the latter sort of principle is open to all the traditional questions about the nature and justification of moral principles.   D. H. Monro, *Empricism and Ethics* (London: Cambridge University Press, 1967), pp. 204-6.

[21] Hare, *Freedom and Reason,* pp. 139-40.

[22] Monro, *Empriricism and Ethics,* p. 204

[23] Ibid., p. 15.

Chapter Seven

Edgar's Having Reasons And Giving Reasons to Others

I continue my clarification of the unique agency of Edgar Egoist by focusing in this chapter upon Edgar's reasoning and upon his giving reasons to other persons. In the case of Edgar's own egoistic program, I will discuss how Edgar gives reasons to himself, better stated as his having or considering reasons for himself. In the case of Edgar's giving reasons to others: I will discuss (1) whether he does so; (2) if he does so, what is the nature of these reasons; and (3) how these reasons are different from the reasons he has for his own egoistic judgments.

In this chapter I will also discuss two related topics regarding the status of Edgar's position insofar as it is normative: this discussion will begin with the question whether Edgar's position is a normative one at all; and I will also discuss in what sense it is not normative. Secondly, I will discuss further universalizability as a feature of giving reasons, raising again the challenge of the consistency of Edgar's program. The product of these discussions will be to bring the clarification of Edgar's agency to a sufficient point, so that we will be conceptually equipped to offer in Chapter Eight the framework for a solution to my question "why should I be moral rather than be an egoist like Edgar?"

The key to my discussion of Edgar Egoist's reasons for action is the same central point in my discussion of Edgar's use of normative language—the role of the egoist's master concept with its egoistic imperative and *agent-anschauung*. As an amoralist, Edgar rejects the fundamental validity of intersubjective normative rules that other people and institutions claim apply commonly to himself and others. And, insofar as Edgar remains a genuine amoral egoist, and does not have a "change of heart," *all* his reasons for what he, Edgar, ought to do are grounded in his egoistic imperative. As such, all Edgar's reasons for his serious "ought" judgments apply to himself alone; his egoistic concept and system is designed for the exclusive guidance of one agent only. If Edgar establishes rules of thumb or constitutive rules for guiding his action in difficult circumstances, the choice and application of such rules will similarly be based upon his egoistic imperative. If Edgar's wants and goals change over time, or circumstances necessitate a significant reevaluation of his relative ability and power to act, his applications of both his egoistic imperative and his supplementary rules may change in interesting ways. However, as a genuine amoral personal egoist, Edgar's reasoning will remain procedurally the same, based exclusively upon his fundamental normative principle.

To facilitate my discussion of whether, and how, Edgar Egoist gives reasons to others, I raise *two related objections*. Both objections arise from my discussion of Edgar Egoist's normative-language use in Chapter Six and in earlier chapters. If Edgar's egoism is unlike any other egoistic account, in being thoroughly personal and secretive, involving a conceptual unity and perception that utilizes a special use of "egoistic ought" in providing exclusive single-agent guidance, then can Edgar Egoist avoid both of the following two characterizations of his position: (a) that Edgar must claim that his normative language comprises a private language unintelligible to any other person, and (b) that Edgar must deny that he can give any reasons at all to others and therefore must face the social inefficiencies of this glaring omission in his everyday practices?

THE PRIVATE LANGUAGE UNINTELLIGIBILITY OBJECTION

The objection that is based on the former characterization makes use of Wittgenstein's discussion of private language in the *Investigations*. If Edgar Egoist's normative language is private language in the sense of "... sounds which no one else understands ...,"[1] then, of course, the appeal of Edgar's position is nil from both a practical and theoretical point of view, since it would then be unintelligible to any other person. Second, if Edgar's language is private in this stronger sense, then the appropriate question to ask about Edgar's complete program of special "egoistic ought" use is "Well, and what of it?"[2] But I argue that Edgar's special language program is both intelligible and has obvious practical implications with considerable consequences for human happiness. The key to avoiding the characterizations of this objection centers on answers to these questions: in what senses is Edgar's normative language private and in what senses is it not private?

To say that Edgar Egoist's normative position is a unique one with a novel use of normative language need not mean that Edgar fails to make use of our common language and that he invents new definitions for all of his own words. In using the term "egoistically ought," for example, in describing how Edgar would guide his actions, I have simply adapted previously understood terms to a special combined use within the clarified concept of an amoral personal egoist. Edgar's use of "egoistically ought" is private in the sense of secretly used; Edgar would not knowingly use this expression socially for fear of tipping off to other agents that he is an egoist. The very reason for Edgar's being secretive and deceptive is that he does not wish to share that which is intelligible to others. If his language were private, in the sense of thoroughly unintelligible to others, then, of course, he would not have to be careful in talking aloud about the application of his egoistic program. In short, for efficiency reasons grounded directly in his fundamental egoistic principle, Edgar must be careful in traffic using his normative language, language that is intelligible in the sense that others can come to understand how he is using the terms, if given careful explanation. His plan is to systematically *not* share the full egoistic meaning of some key first-person, normative language uses, which he has adopted for his own self-directed egoistic guidelines. Another way of accurately stating that Edgar's normative language is private is in the sense of "it is no one else's business," by systematic normative decision as to the limitation of agents to which the normative position applies. The egoistic program is for Edgar alone.

I turn now to two illustrations to further my point that Edgar's normative language is an intelligible adaptation of existing normative language. In one situational example, his son Egbert overhears him saying "I ought to egoistically do X" or "I ought to do Y which is egoistically correct," and Egbert tries to understand what is meant. If Egbert confronts Edgar and explicitly requests an explanation for these uses, Edgar can refer to different common normative uses and discuss alternative combinations. In fact, to maintain his secrecy, Edgar may try to throw Egbert off his normative path by focusing on an inaccurate description of Edgar's use of the key terms, taking advantage of common uses by non-egoists in his characteristic attempt to mislead.[3]

ENLISTING A CONSULTANT FOR CALCULATION EFFICIENCY

In a second example, I imagine Edgar enlisting a consultant to advise him with his tactics and calculations. In theory, like the most efficient tax adviser who knows about one's complete financial situation, one might make the case that the most helpful egoistic calculation consultant is she who knows all about Edgar, not only his prioritized wants and needs, but also that he is a certain sort of egoist and that he uses such and such strategy. Now, it is difficult to imagine a situation in which it would be in Edgar's self-interest to take on such a consultant; but, for purposes of illustration, let me assume that in a certain situation, Edgar is willing to take a risk on a consultant of whom Edgar is confident both that he (Edgar) can control her and that he can read the consultant as to whether she is trying to deceive Edgar or give Edgar the honest advice he wants. The important point in this hypothetical example is that, while it may never be egoistically efficient to enlist a consultant, Edgar's efficiency decision about revealing his agency or not has nothing to do with the intelligibility of what Edgar is reluctant to reveal.

This hypothetical consultant example is also helpful in clarifying what I mean when I say that within Edgar's program "egoistic correctness" or "egoistically right" is limited or restricted to one person alone, Edgar Egoist. By this I mean only that within his egoistic system "egoistic correctness" *applies* by definition only *to* the actions and judgments of one agent. Distinct from this limitation about to whose actions "egoistic correctness" is applied, is the separate question about *by whom* is "egoistic correctness" properly *judged.* On the latter question, Edgar Egoist himself need not be the exclusive and only judge in applying his egoistic imperative, although he would be the only judge by default in every case except those in which he brings in assistance.

With a consultant, Edgar can say that he thought A was the egoistically correct choice, but he was mistaken as to the best application of his egoistic imperative given his prioritized wants and goals. Two examples of applications in which his consultant may be better able to apply his egoistic imperative would be (a) situations in which Edgar is emotionally involved and his judgment clouded and (b) situations in which his egoistic applications may involve a means-end efficiency question which Edgar is not himself qualified to answer, or at least is less qualified to answer than his consultant.

Even without a full-fledged consultant, Edgar can be said to make egoistic errors and also to make use of the efficiency judgments of others. If Edgar judges that he egoistically ought to do X or that X is the egoistically correct thing to do based upon an efficiency calculation that is mistaken, then in retrospect Edgar may see the mistaken assumption about what consequences in fact follow from what conditions or causes; and then Edgar can judge that the overall egoistic judgment, which makes use of his egoistic imperative and his prioritized goals, was egoistically incorrect due to the use of a mistaken means-ends efficiency judgment.

Also Edgar can seek the advice of experts or better qualified resource people by isolating the efficiency question out of the context of his egoistic goals, so that the advice seeking by Edgar is *not recognized* by others *as* part of an egoistic judgment program. Then Edgar can take this efficiency research of options and plug it into his egoistic procedure, which then focuses on what is egoistically necessary (or best, or correct) within his private (for him only) program. However, it is important to emphasize that although Edgar's egoistic judgments, both forward-looking and past-evaluating, may make use of the efficiency expertise of others, by procedural definition the more specific questions about what is *egoistically* correct, etc., applies to Edgar Egoist alone; it is his normative program only.

CAN EDGAR GIVE ANY REASONS TO OTHERS?

I turn now to the second objection above, that Edgar Egoist can give no reasons at all *to others*; and, therefore, the objection states, Edgar's position must admit the practical inefficiencies resulting from this glaring social practice. My reply to this second objection will have two stages. In stage one, I simply offer an explication of how Edgar Egoist would give reasons to others, and hence avoid the social consequences of a strange prohibition. The second stage of this reply will involve raising again the question of univer-salizability and thereby a key challenge to Edgar's consistency. The key point is to show *why* it is that Edgar can consistently give normative reasons for others *to others*. Accordingly, I will first present Edgar's reason-giving practices in a simplified presentation and then turn to further objections, including important consistency challenges, to provide greater clarifying detail.

Of all the reasons that Edgar gives to other persons, it is helpful to distinguish between two primary kinds: (1) explanatory reasons, reasons intended to explain events; and (2) normative reasons, reasons which are intended to guide or influence the actions of others. The former explanatory reasons of Edgar for the most part would differ not at all from the explanatory reasons that non-egoists give to others—honest, straightforward attempts[4] to explain events in terms of causes or conditions.

Of course, it is Edgar's *normative reasons* to others for what they ought to do that are the most interesting reasons given to others. As I have discussed at length, Edgar has no primary concern for how (any) other persons ought to act because as a personal egoist the domain of or limit to his fundamental normative principle is in guiding himself alone; and as an amoralist Edgar rejects as not valid and not applicable to him any other normative guidelines, rules, or principles that claim to guide both himself and (any) others in a common way. However, in social traffic, I suggest that Edgar does not have to be totally mute to the secondary guidance of others, and in fact can consistently engage in a practice of "smoke screen" and manipulative reason-giving to others in order to increase the efficiency of and minimize hindrances to his egoistic program.

In Chapter Six I discussed how, with his "triple-think" approach, Edgar offers "ought"-statement guidance to others, such as, "Egbert and his friends ought to develop the discipline to maintain healthy, drug-free bodies." In expressing such an "ought"-statement Edgar deceptively conceals its corresponding antecedent, "If Egbert and his friends are to be the most useful resource persons for my long-range egoistic goals." This kind of antecedent is for Edgar a *reason for himself* for the normative guidance of others. The antecedent provides a connecting reason to his egoistic imperative. Now when Edgar gives a reason to others *for those others*, this reason-giving is part of a different ball game. In giving reasons to others for the normative guidance of these others, Edgar is not doing either of the following: (1) Edgar is not presenting a reason for normative guidance to a fellow participant within a common normative system; and (2) Edgar is not extending his egoistic system beyond its self-defined limits of applying to one agent only.

What Edgar is doing in giving reasons to Egbert or any other person is at bottom one or the other, or both, of the following two things: (1) Edgar is camouflaging, smoke-screening, avoiding suspicion that he is secretly an amoral egoist; and/or (2) he is manipulating these other persons so that they unwittingly assist, or at least do not frustrate, Edgar in furthering his egoistic program. In short, to use sports terminology, Edgar can give normative reasons to others: (a) for defensive purposes, to defend the secrecy of his egoistic agency, or (b) for offensive tactical ends, to use others to achieve Edgar's own egoistic goals. Regarding Edgar's defensive tactics, when he is in a normative discussion[5] with others, Edgar may proceed in either of two common ways: Edgar may attempt to stop discussion or at least his role in the discussion by appealing to some rule of customary morality that is widely accepted, for example, "Be a good example for your children," thereby attempting to avoid the tough questions; or (2) Edgar may attempt to shift the focus of discussion from a concern about "correct" (for others) value principles to a concern with factual questions that have to do with applying various principles, for example, *de facto* questions about the maintenance of the body's health.

On the offensive side, Edgar's use of manipulative reason-giving to others will, as with all his judgments, depend on efficiency judgments (what can be gained or lost) given his prioritized goals; however, for the most part Edgar will very much limit this sort of reason-giving to others, in order to maintain the simplicity of his program. To engage in much manipulative reason-giving to others is to invite the greater probability of others questioning his reasons offered. And the greater the questioning, (1) the greater will the focus be on Edgar himself and (2) the greater will be the effort required to explain the consistency and relation between his different reasons (to others), and (3) the greater chance of Edgar's making a mistake and revealing his agency.

At this point, I want to clarify a question of consistency, not among the group itself of reasons given to others by Edgar, but the consistency question regarding how Edgar's first-person, seriously prescribed "ought"-judgments are consistent with his second- and third-person manipulative and concealment "ought"-judgments to others.   This particular question is not, and need not be, a problematic one for Edgar. The reason this consistency question is not problematic is that the two uses of "ought," the first-person egoistically prescribed "ought" and the second- and third-person reason-giving-to-others "ought" are entirely different in their use, comprising entirely different illocutionary functions. Given Edgar's unique agency, which by definition has absolutely no interest or commitment to participating in an honest exhibition of common normative evaluation and guidance with others, procedurally built into Edgar's program are two different sorts of guidance for very different ends. And, as I will soon discuss at greater length, Edgar sees no point in fussing about a consistency matter which may make sense to moralists, who do not define such disparity[6] between themselves and the agency of others.

EDGAR'S CONSISTENCY CONCERNS

Starting from the top, Edgar has two main consistency concerns. On the one hand, his primary consistency concern is to maintain a systematic egoistic system of thought and action that can be articulated consistently for his own clarity. The advantage of which is that he is an efficiency-minded egoist without the confusions and hindrances of having inconsistent thought and goals. Clearness of his egoistic thought is necessary for his definiteness of purpose and in keeping in sight his prioritized goals.

The second consistency concern is in the limited area of giving "ought" reasons to others, for egoistically designed manipulative or concealment purposes. Edgar's concern here is simply a matter of keeping the manipulation talk all straight so that he does not get in trouble with his resource people. Trouble arises if he is requested to give more reasons; by giving more reasons he focuses others' attention on himself, and perhaps the nature of his agency. But the clever Edgar will take the maxim, if you can't say anything (to others) efficiently (of course, by Edgar's standards), then do not say anything at all.

Unlike an amoral personal egoist like Edgar, the moralist will be concerned that his first-person reasons for "ought"-statements are consistent with his reasons for second- and third-person "ought"-statements. Unlike the deceptive Edgar, Mike Moralist gives reasons to others, as he gives them for himself, attempting to present his reasons with clarity and honesty, and assuming his reasons, at least in morally relevant situations, apply, if he is correct, to others in a common practice of evaluating the actions of fellow moral agents, participating in a common normative system. With Edgar no common normative system of evaluation is assumed or accepted at all. In serious normative reason-giving, there is for Edgar only first-person, egoistic reason-giving. This is the only normative system that he accepts. Any normative reason-giving offered by Edgar in support of second- and third-person "ought"-statements performs an entirely different function than it does for Mike Moralist. For Edgar this reason-giving functions as deceptive manipulation, a tactical ploy offered for egoistic reasons, *without* and not within any larger common evaluation system with which he must check his own egoistic reason-having. In short, for Edgar the whole ball game is egoistic first-person reason-having; other reasons may be useful tools in traffic but have no validity in that system which is the only (egoistic) game in town.

IS EDGAR'S POSITION A NORMATIVE ONE AT ALL?

I will expand on this discussion of Edgar's consistency by considering some important objections to the claim of egoistic consistency, including some further discussion of universalizability. However, this is the place to pull some of my descriptions of Edgar Egoist together and consider an important question, the answering of which will add much to my characterization of Edgar's agency. The question is, in what sense (or senses) is Edgar's egoism normative at all; and, the other side of the same coin, in what sense (or senses) is the position not normative? I prepare the clarification of the question as follows: Given that Edgar's serious normative guidance is limited to one person and does not really extend to any other persons, and given that any ethical discussion that Edgar may reluctantly engage in is not an honest and genuine participation, but an exercise in manipulation, and given that Edgar is not at all committed to a common justificatory procedure or ethical truth, the question is: How can Edgar's amoral personal egoism correctly be characterized as a normative position at all? I lay out my answers to these questions by considering in turn Edgar's egoism first as a theory, secondly as a defensible position, thirdly as normative in various senses, and finally by contrasting my account of Edgar with the approach and assumptions of Henry Sidgwick in his *Methods of Ethics.*

In his now classic article, "Ultimate Principles and Ethical Egoism," Brian Medlin reminds us that the egoist who cannot promulgate his doctrine has no doctrine at all.[7] Similarly, if one understands a normative theory, in its barest essentials, as a theory which offers a single procedure or principle for the common guidance of each of the members of *a group* of persons in their interactions with one another, the amoral egoist's position is no normative theory at all, for no common guidance nor a single procedure is offered for more than one person.

If one cannot call Edgar Egoist's position a normative theory in any significant sense, in what sense is it a normative *position* at all? If not a theory, is it a normative commitment that is defensible as an argumentative position? In considering this characterization, we want to remember that an amoral egoist like Edgar would never in practice defend his fundamental principle or egoistic commitment as the best for himself, much less for anyone else—such an attempt would blatantly violate his policy of maintaining secrecy, thereby being practically self-defeating or egoistically inefficient.

A distinct question is the following: Even if a genuine egoist would never defend amoral egoism in practice, is it nevertheless an argumentative position that is *in principle* defensible as a fundamental principle? But what would it mean for an amoral egoist to argumentatively defend his normative stance, independent of the above consideration of consequences? Would doing so make any sense for Edgar? As an amoralist, Edgar certainly would not defend it as morally right. As a categorical egoist, neither would Edgar defend his position for some other ends, such as because his egoism would bring the greatest happiness to the greatest number. At this point it is helpful to emphasize an important void in Edgar's normative posture, the absence of any ethical participation with others, even in his own thought. Given Edgar's *agent-anschauung* with his lack of good will, his lack of interest in any honest participation in ethical justification, in short, his absence of genuine respect for any other ethical agents, much less their practices, the question of whether Edgar can defend his position loses point. To ask whether Edgar can even swing the bat, much less get a base hit in someone's ethical game that Edgar has no use for, is not a very interesting question, especially when he never *really* steps on the field, so to speak. And, of course, if in social traffic Edgar finds himself forced to talk in a discussion of justification or normative truth, Edgar will simply make one or more of his defensive moves or simply take the situation as an opportunity for manipulation.

Therefore, the term "position" as used commonly in ethics to refer to candidates for interpersonal argumentative evaluation does not apply. I refer hereafter to the egoist's commitment as a normative "posture," for one may say that Edgar Egoist holds a normative position in the weaker sense of "position," as that which is posited, whether or not it is posited on the ethical table, or whether it is argumentatively defensible, or not. Although not a competitive candidate in the rough and tumble of normative discourse, if I have been both accurate and realistic in my account of Edgar's amoral personal egoism, one can without confusion be such an egoist, that is, hold that normative posture. Furthermore, although Edgar's agency is void of any commitment to a common ethics, yet insofar as he concerns himself with value judgments and action guidance according to principle, however restrictive in scope and purpose, there is a minimal sense in which this egoistic posture is normative.

Although this amoral egoistic account may be called normative in this weaker sense, it is also importantly not normative in the stronger sense of normative, as rule following, etc. of a certain sort, namely as a member of a common ethical community with common normative commitments. Henry Sidgwick in *The Methods of Ethics* writes, that "the special and distinct aim" of ethics and politics is to systematically attempt to determine what human conduct is right and which of the divergent judgments about the former is valid.[8] In the last paragraph of this same introduction, Sidgwick says,

> My object, then, in the present work, is to expound as clearly and as fully as my limits will allow the different methods of Ethics that I find implicit in our common moral reasoning; to point out their mutual relations; and where they seem to conflict, to define the issue as much as possible.[9]

By contrast, Edgar Egoist's posture does not add to Sidgwick's study a new or different method of ethics. This amoral personal egoist is *not* just a strange new method of how *we* ought to act in a common ethical system. It is a-ethical or "ethics-less." Although it has method and system within its own self-defined limitations, Edgar's egoism falls outside the scope of Sidgwick's study and beyond the limits of any common ethical community.

EDGAR'S REASONS ARE NOT JUSTIFICATORY REASONS

In the remainder of the chapter, I attend to differentiating between (1) how Edgar Egoist has egoistic reasons for himself, (2) how Edgar Egoist gives some manipulative reasons to others, and (3) how both (1) and (2) are distinct from how the non-egoist gives justificatory reasons to other non-egoists. To this end, I turn to the careful writing of Alan Gewirth and some key discussions of universalizability, "ought"-use, reason-giving, and consistency.

In Chapter Six, I argued that the linguistically astute Edgar Egoist can consistently meet the demands of universalizability in the sense of (U2), that is, he can both communicate consistently and remain a full-fledged egoist, albeit a secret one. The reason the egoist a la (U2) can consistently apply his egoistic discrimination is that (U2) allows the egoistic maker of an "ought"-judgment the freedom to define the original grounds for the judgment, and therefore the "relevant respects" in which other "ought"-judgments are similar to it. According to Alan Gewirth's more stringent universalizability thesis such variability and freedom in one's universalizing grounds are ruled out. In "Must One Play the Moral Language Game?" Gewirth warns his readers:

> The phrase "X universalizes his 'ought'-statements may be misleading if it suggests that the universalizability of an 'ought'-statement is at the option of the speaker. For a singular 'ought'-statement necessarily implies a universal statement, regardless of whether the speaker admits this; ... X's statement, (S) "I ought to do Z because I want to have Y," is enthymematic; it entails the suppressed major: (U) "All persons who want to have Y ought to do Z."[10]

That provision which provides the teeth in Gewirth's universalizability thesis appears in a more explicit statement in the second footnote of his article, "The Non-Trivializability of Universalizability."

> According to the universalizability thesis, a singular moral judgment, which says that some individual S has some moral predicate P, is based on a reason according to which (a) S has some non-moral property Q and (b) having Q is a *sufficient justifying* condition for having P, so that

if one accepts the judgment and the reason then one must accept the generalization that every subject that has Q has P. [Emphasis mine.][11]

The distinct contribution of Gewirth's account of universalizability—let us call it *justificatory universalizability* (JU)— I take to be the provision that a universalization-relevant reason must be accepted both as a *sufficient* reason and as a *justificatory* reason. It is this crucial twofold provision which gives JU the stringency to rule out discriminatory universalizing in justificatory arguments, but careful attention to this same twofold provision shows that JU may not apply at all to an egoistic agent like Edgar.

I turn first to the justificatory aspect of JU. In applying JU as a consistency test for the egoist's use of normative language, it is important to note that the linguistically astute Edgar never attempts to justify his actions to others or for others or as a serious move within a common practice of justifying. In statement (S) "I ought to do Z because I want to have Y," Edgar Egoist never uses "because" as presenting a candidate for justification. As an amoral egoist, Edgar rejects not only the content of morality, but also such ethical practices and mental habits as common normative truth-seeking and the interpersonal legitimatizing of reasons for acting. Edgar certainly agrees that, if one utters a statement of the form S above, and one means (and is taken to mean) thereby that "because I want to have Y" is a sufficient justificatory reason, presented for intersubjective criticism and acceptability, then one is logically committed on pain of contradiction to accept the similar wants of others as sufficiently justifying as well. One of the ways in which Edgar parts company with those of us who do not share his fundamental normative position is in refusing to take that first justificatory step of offering any ethical justifications at all.

Along similar lines, while discussing egoism, Bernard Williams notes that, "What he (the egoist) would not be rational in saying is that it is all right for him, but not all right for others."[12] After a discussion of "What is special about you?" Williams concludes,

... and similarly, it may be said, the question will still remain whether what he is doing is all right, even if he refuses to consider it. What that objection says is not altogether wrong, in the sense that it rightly makes the point that whether moral concepts apply to the egoist's projects is not just a function of whether the egoist wants them to. But it does not get us any further in arguing with him, since we knew already that he was declining to measure the world by moral notions by which others do measure it; what was needed was an argument to show that he gets into intellectual trouble in so refusing.   That is not provided by the insistence that the 'all right' question does apply—it merely reiterates that he ought not to refuse.[13]

It is in a similar vein that Edgar does not ethically justify his actions.

However, if an egoist like Sam Snake, as linguistically clumsy as Edgar is astute, were to attempt to justify his egoistic "ought"-judgments to the ethical community with the claim that his (and only his) reasons were unique, and therefore that they were unable to generate a generalization that applies to other persons also, such an attempt at the individualization objection would fail. For, as Gewirth argues, if one claims a unique property in justification of one's special claim to a given moral predicate, by reason of being named Sam S. Snake, for example, then other persons may claim similar unique properties in a proportional or relational way, for example by being named Tilly Trivializability. "The diversity of the relata does not affect the sameness of the relation nor, to that extent, the sameness of the reason."[14]   Why it is that these personal reasons similarly related to their authors are accurately called "the same reason" is due to the fact that they are presented as justifications. Sam Snake must either give up altogether trying to justify his egoistically defined "ought"-judgments, like Edgar, or he will keep finding himself ending up in one inconsistency after another when his alleged "personal" justifying reasons are brought to the test of Gewirth's carefully stated universalizability principle, JU.

Another mistaken move that Sam Snake can make within the practice of justification is to appeal to the individualistic axiom, "I ought to do X simply because I am I."   In his penetrating article, "Ethical Egoism Reconsidered," George Carlson discusses this individualistic axiom in the context of evaluating J. A. Brunton's attempt to place egoism on the logical map:[15]

> ... I should still want to argue my central thesis, namely, that the "mere otherness" of each agent cannot logically justify restricting the individualistic axiom to oneself. I say this, because everyone is "merely other." "Mere otherness" tendered as an excepting condition is therefore reiterable with respect to all agents ..., which is to say that it is logically no excepting condition at all.[16]

Surely if Sam Snake were to attempt to justify or defend his judgment "I ought to do X" with "because I am I," Sam's claim within the practice of ethical justification is "no excepting condition at all."

How Edgar Egoist functions differently than Sam Snake is that Edgar never sincerely participates by thought or action in any common practices of justification. In analyzing Brunton, Carlson writes that Brunton's discussion of "personal experiences," "... does highlight the psychological aspects of 'mere otherness' and the uniqueness of selfhood; it does not, however, provide a rational warrant for excepting oneself from the moral pale ... ."[17] Contrary to Sam Snake, Edgar Egoist never does seek any interpersonal warrant or legitimatization for what he does or for whether his posture is within or without the moral pale.

To return to Alan Gewirth's argument in "Must One Play the Moral Language Game?" the qustion whether a prescriptive "ought"-statement "I ought to do Z" entails a universal statement, also prescriptive, such as "All persons who want to have Y ought to do Z" depends upon two importantly related assumptions: (1) that the use of "ought" in the first-person "ought"-statement is such that the necessity prescribed is of the sort that applies to all persons and is not restricted to the domain of one agent; and (2) that the reason-giving used in support of the first-person "ought"-statement is presented as a justificatory reason that is deemed sufficient by the speaker. It is due to the unique normative posture of Edgar Egoist that neither of these common assumptions apply to him. First of all, when Edgar is seriously prescribing an S statement, in application of his egoistic program, the statement can only be correctly understood as "I egoistically ought to do Z," with the range, applicability, and character of the required action guidance being restrictively determined. Secondly, Edgar Egoist's uses of "because" when they follow such prescribed S statements never involve an honest presentation of a candidate for justification.

Edgar may consider reasons *within* the egoistic program (of course, for himself only), in terms of providing an egoistic ground for S in either of two ways: (1) by appealing to a more basic egoistic rule or principle of which S is an application; or (2) by appealing to a strategic reading of a factual situation which will significantly affect the applicability of one or more egoistic rules or principles. In either case Edgar is giving reasons for himself alone due to the nature of his egoistic agency.

To summarize the above, although the amoral egoist cannot, without contradicting himself, defend his unique normative posture as justified, right, or correct in a non-egoistic interpersonal sense while still remaining a true amoral egoist; yet, with the proper linguistic, illocutionary, and methodological restrictions and adjustments, a careful egoist like Edgar can judge and act with full consistency (albeit with considerable secrecy and deceit also) in a world peopled with non-egoists. However, due to the egoist's extreme illocutionary and justificatory restrictions for consistency in action and planning, Alan Gewirth's justificatory universalizability principle (JU) fails to capture the careful egoist in consistency problems. It is the strengths of Gewirth's JU thesis, with its emphasis on justification, so central to moral philosophy, and its explicitness of statement, that allow an amoral personal egoist like Edgar to sidestep its application.[18]

In Chapters Six and Seven, I have attempted to lay out the normative language use, as well as the reason-having and reason-giving practices, of that genuine practical alternative to being moral—the life of Edgar Egoist. I have attempted to free this character from much unwarranted criticism on grounds of a lack of linguistic conformity or of a lack of logical and systematic consistency. At the same time my account of Edgar Egoist has set the stage for discussing the more fundamental and systematic problems that now arise once one has articulated Edgar's language-use, reasoning and social planning with the sophistication and adaptability to handle the first-order challenges to his agency.

We are now prepared to turn in Chapter Eight to a discussion of the groundwork or basics for preparing an answer to the question I have framed, "Why should I be moral rather than be an amoral personal egoist?" We are now in a position to articulate an answer that is neither mired in needless confusion nor disappointing in its superficiality, the latter being inappropriate to the tough complexity of such life-defining judgments.

Notes

[1] Ludwig Wittgenstein, *Philosophical Investigations*, trans. G.E.M. Anscombe (New York: Macmillan Co., 1953), p. 94.

[2] Ibid.

3   For a very different use of Wittgenstein's private language argument, see Christine Korsgaard's Part V of her Lecture Three from Cambridge University's November, 1992, Tanner Lectures on Human Values. Her Tanner Lectures "The Sources of Normativity" will be published along with commentary by Cambridge University Press. Korsgaard argues in an imaginative way that all humans, even the egoist, take the reasons of others into account. The key question is, *in what sense or senses* does an Edgar Egoist take the reasons of his human resources into account? Is it the same sense in which Mike Moralist values the reasoning process and products of his fellow respected moral agents?

   In the very last section of Part V in Lecture Three (3.5.11) Korsgaard predicts "... the myth of egoism will die with the myth of the privacy of consciousness." With a big grin, Edgar Egoist says *to himself*, "That is just the kind of thinking that I myself would selectively choose to share with others in the crowd that I work."

4   I can think of two kinds of exceptions to this general account of explanatory reasons which Edgar might make for his own advantage: (1) in situations in which Edgar's own interests can be seriously affected by Edgar's explanatory account, if honestly given; and (2) in situations in which Edgar is requested to explain his own reasoning for why in fact he did X, a request for first-person motivational reasons.

5   Edgar's normative discussions will not be genuine efforts in the sense of serious and honest participation, but only apparently so, if he is successfully efficient. Having different ends, Edgar will make a different use of the opportunity than his interlocutors who share among themselves honesty and sincerity with a common normative goal or set of goals.

6   For an interesting discussion of the egoist's disparity in thinking about others, see Thomas Nagel's discussion of dissociation in his *The Possibility of Altruism* (Princeton: Princeton University Press, 1970), esp. chaps. XI and XII.

7   Medlin, "Ultimate Principles and Ethical Egoism," p. 58.

8   Sidgwick, *Methods of Ethics*, p. 2.

9   Ibid., p. 14.

10   Alan Gewirth, "Must One Play the Moral Language Game?" *American Philosophical Quarterly* 7 (1970): 112.

11   Alan Gewirth, "The Non-Trivializability of Universalizability," *Australasian Journal of Philosophy* 47 (1969): 123.

12   Williams, *Problems of the Self*, p. 254.

13 Ibid., p. 255.

14 Gewirth, "Non-Trivializability," p. 129.

15 Brunton, "Egoism and Morality," pp. 289-303, reprinted in Margolis, *Contemporary Ethical Theory*, pp. 280-300.

As I understand Brunton's article, his main concern is to "fix (egoism's) place on the logical map." Carlson's conclusion, that "... Brunton has failed to provide sufficient cause rationally to vindicate ethical egoism in its individual rendering ..." (p. 33) may imply Brunton's failing in more than he attempted to do. From Edgar Egoist's viewpoint, as Brunton, Gewirth, and other philosophers work out the logical map for accepted uses of "ought," "right," "because," etc., Edgar will, in typical parasitic fashion, extend some of those uses, such as "egoistically ought," in order to articulate for himself how his egoistic system works. Perhaps one can correctly say then that Edgar has tangentially developed a small logic of novel terminology that is special to his system, that only he is interested in developing and using.

16 Carlson, "Ethical Egoism Reconsidered," p. 32.

17 Ibid.

18 For another look at how Alan Gewirth argues that the amoral egoist implicitly contradicts himself, see his tightly argued book, *Reason and Morality*, esp. pp. 78-95.

Part IV

The Framework
for an Answer

Chapter Eight

The Egoist's Human Costs and Theoretical Liabilities

In the first seven chapters I have offered an articulation of the question "Why should I be moral?" in a way that tries to do justice to the complexity of life itself and its choices, and more specifically, to what is actually involved in an agent's making this kind of fundamental normative acceptance. I call this basic question a question of first-person acceptability.

One can raise this question either from within the perception or *agent-anschauung* of an amoral egoist, like Edgar, or from outside this perception, from a non-egoistic or moral point of view. The first-person acceptability question from the former point of view can be raised in this fashion: "Ought I *continue* to be an amoral personal egoist?" Or one may be egoistic but undisciplined and sloppy, and ask oneself something like, "Ought I to get serious and really be an amoral personal egoist in a consistent and disciplined way?" A second way that the first-person acceptability question can be raised is from outside the egoistic stance and then the focus is on the appeal or attractiveness of an unfamiliar viewpoint one does not now share.

I will argue in this chapter that to entrench oneself in a life of amoral personal egoism is to pay a considerable price in both practical and theoretical considerations. From the point of its appeal to us non-egoists, a careful evaluation must include these practical and theoretical disadvantages. But, before laying out these key considerations, let us first consider what is involved in answering this first-person acceptability question. To get an interesting start on this difficult matter, I now look at two positions about acceptability which hold that at this fundamental level one is no longer dealing with argumentative considerations, but *only* arbitrary choice.

FIRST-PERSON ACCEPTABILITY
AS AN ARBITRARY CHOICE

In Chapter Two I discussed the position of Paul Taylor on this "ultimate question." Taylor states that no reasons can be given which provide an answer to the question "Why should I be moral?" One just decides to be a certain kind of person.

> No argument can be given to show that his decision is irrational or that it is based on false assumptions ... . Commitment to moral principles, then, is finally a matter of one's will, not of one's reason ... . Reason alone cannot tell us what choice to make. We must not expect, therefore, that someone might provide us with an argument showing which alternative ought to be chosen. There is simply no way to evade the responsibility—a responsibility that rests upon each of us alone—for defining our own selves.[1]

I contrasted this view of Taylor's with that of Plato, who never considers abandoning the presumption that discourse and argument are necessary, if not sufficient, ingredients for showing which ultimate choice makes one happier and showing which same choice exhibits knowledge, and which exhibits ignorance. Plato agrees with Taylor that answering an ultimate question such as "Why should I be moral?" is a matter of individual choice, in the sense that for this sort of choice each person herself cannot truly evade responsibility. However, in contrast to Taylor, Plato holds that, not only are there personal risks and consequences for such a choice, but that there is the personal risk of choosing to be a fool and the possibility of being mistaken and ignorant even on this fundamental sort of question. It is in the spirit of Plato's presumption, that discussion and argument both make sense and are not in vain at this basic normative level, that I present a final chapter about a framework for a solution to the question.

Another who takes the position that an answer to such a fundamental question is a matter of arbitrary choice is Henry David Aiken. Aiken holds that the question "Why should I be moral?" is a question beyond the level of ethical discourse, beyond the reach of any philosophical discussion to answer.

> Such questions have no single answer, nor is there any criterion save interest itself which can determine when an answer to the question is satisfactory. I am "satisfied" and the question is "answered" not when some objective conditions have been met but when my practical indecision or doubt has been removed—when, that is to say, I have been provided with an adequate motive for playing the moral game.[2]

According to Aiken, then, there are only subjective and individual answers that each person can give to such a question. Like the question, "Why should I do anything?" such a question is "beyond reason" and can only be answered by each normative agent in a free, "gratuitous decision," untethered to any given theoretical framework.

My response to Taylor and Aiken touches on a good part of what I have accomplished in the above chapters. If I am correct in capturing the complexity of being an agent like Edgar Egoist, then (to use Taylor's terminology) the "full meaning" of one's choice to be like Edgar Egoist or the process of "defining oneself" as such an egoist involves a complexity that can not be successfully accounted for by the philosophical psychology assumed by Taylor and Aiken. I suggest that the appropriate model for what is truly involved in such a fundamental, first-person acceptability question, such as, "Why should I be moral rather than like an Edgar Egoist?" is *not* that of an arbitrary choice, *not* a choice beyond the realm of philosophic discussion and criticism.

If I am correct, some important consequences follow which are helpful in evaluating views like those of Taylor and Aiken. The first point to make concerns the use of terminology like "choice" and "decision" in referring to this first-person acceptability question. If one characterizes the answering of this fundamental question as a decision or choice, one must admit that this kind of choice is very much not the everyday variety, but rather is uniquely fundamental and normatively and theoretically complex. To "decide" to be like Edgar Egoist is not like choosing from the menu, deciding to be a plumber, nor even choosing the right mate.

In assenting to a life of egoism, Edgar Egoist assents to a master concept which involves an *agent-anschauung* of himself *vis-a-vis* all other normative agents; and this master concept unifies his decision-making and strategical planning that runs throughout his practical life. While it is not inconceivable that one could come to assent to the egoistic life (or the moral life) in a spontaneously decisive moment, I suggest that it is mistaken to assume that such an assent, however spontaneous in a special case, is a simple assent that is void of theoretical complications. Furthermore, such assent is normally a gradual process of thought and will, analogous to trying on a suit of clothes and seeing how these clothes "fit," or better yet seeing how they "fit and match." The termination point of the assent process in my analogy will involve the judgment "I'll go with it." In the case of answering the first-person acceptability question, when one judges "I'll go with it," one is assenting to a complex conceptual package which, as I will soon discuss, involves methodological and metaphysical assumptions, as well as normative elements. If one insists on terms like "choosing" amoral egoism, what is involved in such a choice is choosing a conceptual complexity of a certain sort with such and such methodological and metaphysical assumptions: a choosing, if you like, in light of a given package of theoretical assumptions.

THE MODEL OF THE SPINNING CARNIVAL SEARCHLIGHT

Of course, the kind of theoretical model one uses to understand this acceptability process is also helpful in evaluating a characterization of the process. Aiken for one says that a question like "Why should I be moral?" is simply a question of whether or not one has sufficient interest in or motive for "playing the moral (or egoistic) game." One almost gets the impression from his language that Aiken's imaginative model for answering the question is the following: that such fundamental assent is like parachuting under the cover of darkness into the center of a carnival or circus, and upon landing turning on a powerful beam of light and arbitrarily spinning this search light, as if it were a spinner on a Las Vegas game board. The analagous completion of one's assent corresponds in this model to the spinning searchlight arbitrarily coming to a stop on one of the entrances to the "games" of life, such as the ball toss or the dart game.

One of the problems with this model is that it assumes no preparation and no deliberation about preparation prior to spinning the searchlight of interest or decision. For this reason I judge it unrealistic and theoretically weak in explanatory usefulness. The following features about human life are relevant to evaluating the limitations of the above imaginative model. In the challenging real world, (a) it is *not* the case that everyone starts in the same position in life nor arrives in the same position prior to one's *single* big life "choice" (analogous to arrival at the center of the carnival); (b) the fundamental acceptability questions in life, involving normative value and theoretical support, are continuously applicable and are not a one-time "choice" (one must be ready at any given time to answer whether one should stay entrenched as one now has entrenched oneself); and (c) most importantly, these continuously applicable acceptability questions can be pushed back prior to a "key decisive moment" and one can raise and attempt to answer the same kind of questions about the value or appropriateness of one's *preparation* or self-development: one's self-education, one's building of character, and the development of one's interests themselves.

For example, one related question is why should I pursue that sort of self-improvement and development of interests which encourage a Christian rather than an egoistic point of view? Life's challenges include not only focusing on the choice of a "game of life," but also the question of how to develop oneself to be best prepared for this game.[3] To return to the imaginative model, analogous to life's challenges is the challenge of how to construct one's own light source and generator and a whole set of rules and habits for its "proper" use—a use program for my tools of will and thought that I can "go with."

An interesting contrast to Taylor and Aiken is the writing of Iris Murdoch who advises her readers to frequently return to the initial descriptive survey of moral phenomena. And, as we do return to the original phenomena, Murdoch warns us to continually reconsider "... what our philosophic techniques actually *do* for us."[4] She goes on to argue that if one characterizes the moral life as simply a series of overt choices in specifiable situations, defensible by criteria-specifiable arguments, one has thereby left out important elements of the original moral phenomena.

> ... when we attend to the notion of "moral being" as self-reflection or complex attitudes to life which are continuously displayed and elaborated in overt and inward speech but are not separable temporally into situations ... here moral differences look less like differences of choice, given the same facts, and more like differences of vision ... . We differ not only because we select different objects out of the same world but because we see different worlds.[5]

I suggest that, unless we arbitrarily exclude for theoretical simplification from our initial description of egoistic phenomena the role of the unifying master concept, as well as the relevant strategy principles and habit formation, assent to the egoistic life rather than the moral life (or the other way around) is more like Murdoch's "differences of vision" than Aiken's spontaneous decisions. How these different normative conceptions in fact develop, could develop, or should develop are important areas of research that I cannot pursue in this work.

Like Plato, I believe that the most interesting and challenging questions have to do not with choices about action or categories of action, but with acceptability questions about being a certain kind of agent. And, if I am correct about what is truly involved in the interesting and challenging agency of Edgar Egoist, such fundamental acceptability involves a conceptual framework and judgment system with considerable complexity, which, as I will show, leaves plenty of room for theoretical assumptions.

My emphasis on agency rather than action and on preparation for decision rather than spontaneity are strikingly exhibited by contrasting my approach to answering the question "Why should I be moral?" with that of Henry David Aiken. Aiken suggests that answering this fundamental first-person acceptability question is like asking a more general question.

> In the end, then, the fundamental human problem is not to provide an answer to the question "Why should I do X?" but "Why should I do anything?" This is a question which is beyond reason. If it is senseless then, as human beings, we are at bottom committed to the posing of senseless questions. Decision is King.[6]

Note that Aiken classifies this beyond-philosophy *human* problem as a matter of "doing" rather than "being," calling for a spontaneous decision or choice. But we have found that to really *do* the egoistic thing *as an egoistic action* involves first of all *being* the egoistic agent, with all the conceptual and normative complexity that it involves. If my clarification and argument is largely correct, then the question "Why should I be moral?" is not like "Why should I do anything" as much as it is like asking: "Why should I *be* anything?"[7] This kind of tough question, understood in its complexity, does not lend itself to a theoretically simplistic, spontaneous choice. At this level of questioning, *everything* is at issue. We do not leave the philosophic arena, arriving in a "human" area free of philosophic considerations. The tough "decisions" such as assenting to *be* moral or to *be* an Edgar Egoist have philosophic threads running throughout. These "human questions" are laden with philosophic turns because human agents and their awareness of life's options are just extremely complex. In answering "Why should I be moral?" or in answering "Why should I *be* anything?" everything is at stake, whether or not a normative agent such as Edgar wants to defend his continually applicable "decision" for entrenchment. Before laying out some of Edgar's theoretical baggage and the practical weight of such baggage, I turn for some interesting background comparisons to the writing of Bernard Williams.

Attending to the work of Bernard Williams will help clarify my account of the amoral personally egoistic option by way of contrast. My differences with Williams in the area of philosophic psychology, egoistic psychology in particular, will be instructive. According to Williams, once one has cleared away some of the consistency challenges, the key question is whether the amoral egoist that remains is sufficiently attractive or appealing as an agent to provide any challenging alternative to the life of morality. If what one has left is a normative agent who is not affected at all by the sufferings or distress of any other person, all one has come up with is a psychopath; but "... the idea of arguing [the psychopath] into morality is surely idiotic, but the fact that it is idiotic has equally no tendency to undermine the basis of morality or rationality."[8] Similarly, Williams notes,

> Of course a man can be consistent by having no, or very few, thoughts; and that some dismal self-seeking brute can satisfy the egoist specification I shall take to be of little interest. The egoist will be more interesting *vis-a-vis* morality if as well as having a fair range of territory to operate in, he should be moreover moderately attractive, where that means moderately attractive to us.[9]

Edgar Egoist as I have described him, is neither an unfeeling psychopath[10] nor a mindless brute. The important question *in what sense* does Edgar have feelings for others, I will confront in a bit, but there is no question that an egoist like Edgar requires considerable intellectual and imaginative powers to make his way.

DISTINGUISHING THE EGOIST FROM THE ALTRUIST

What is most interesting about Williams' account, for my purposes, is how he distinguishes the egoist from the altruist. This distinction for Williams is simply a matter of degree, how far and how often an agent extends his sympathies to other persons.

> The trouble with the egoist is not that it is *desires* that he expresses, nor that they are *his* desires—the trouble is that all his desires are for things *for him* ... . All the egoist's wants are either of the form "I want that

I ...," where this is followed by something which specifies his getting something, entering into a desirable state, or whatever; or else, if they are not of that form they depend on another desire which is of that form, in the sense that it is only because he has that latter desire that he has the former, and that if the latter went away or were satisfied in some other way, the former would go away ... . I shall use the term "I desire" for a desire whose propositional content requires 'I' or related expressions ('my' etc.); and the term 'non-I desire' for one that does not. I shall speak of a *basically* non-I desire, to refer to a non-I desire which does not depend on an I-desire. [11]

Williams uses an example of the desire to help another person named Mary. He argues that, just as an altruist is motivated by the thought "they need help," not by the thought "Mary needs help and I have a desire that she be helped,"

> The structure of our man's thoughts in these respects is in fact no different from the altruist's, nor are either his thoughts or his desires any more concerned with himself than are the altruist's. What is defective with him vis-a-vis the altruist is rather that his non-I benevolent dispositions and desires are so restricted, both because their objects are (relative to their needs) randomly selected, and also because he has no sympathy for others who have non-I desires for persons in whom they are interested. [12]

In chapter one of *Morality: An Introduction to Ethics*, Williams puts the matter this way:

> This is a vital point: this man is capable of thinking in terms of others' interest, and his failure to be a moral agent lies (partly) in the fact that he is only intermittently and capriciously disposed to do so. But there is no bottomless gulf between this state and the basic dispositions of morality. There are people who need help who are not people who at the moment he happens to want to help, or likes; and there are other people who like and want to help other particular people in need. To get him to consider their situation seems rather an extension of his imagination and his understanding, than a discontinuous step onto something quite different, the 'moral plane.' [13]

The question "Why should I be moral?" for Williams is then simply the question, "Why should I extend my sympathies for others (sympathies which I now have) even further, i.e. to more people?" The only question remaining then for the non-egoistic observer of the egoist, and for all interested members of society who may want to minimize egoistic tendencies, is "how?"—"how to extend his sympathies," how to "extend his imagination and understanding," i.e., by what training, education, or motivational program?

Williams' differences from my analysis are extremely helpful in sharpening the edges of the total picture of the amoral personal egoism that I have presented. I have argued that careful description reveals that there is a distinctive gulf, which may be passable by individual agents, between the genuine amoral personal egoist and the life of the non-egoist. The explanation for this gulf in the normative sphere lies with the structure of Edgar Egoist's thought. Edgar's concept of himself as a normative agent of a special sort and his fundamental egoistic principle conceptually package, organize and prioritize his entire normative life in a way that separates himself as distinct among all normative agents. In Williams' terminology, Edgar Egoist has no non-I desires that are basic and also simple, that is, independent of and not subject to a prioritization activity that is in strict application of the egoistic principle. If Edgar desires that Mary be helped, that desire does not appear as a simple, autonomous, separate spring to action, but is fitted into a complex organization of wants related in a distinctive way. In practice, Edgar may articulate his desire that Mary be helped in the following ways: "I desire that Mary be helped by Aunt Suzie's time and energy" or "I desire that Mary be helped with Uncle Waldo's money." Such articulations suggest the actual complexity of helping decisions with the interplay of competing wants and also how a character like Edgar would in fact work toward Mary's being helped.

However, one could think of situations in which Edgar Egoist, upon hearing just a brief communication "Mary needs help," immediately springs to action himself. This may occur because Mary's instrumental value *vis-a-vis* Edgar's careful program of prioritized wants has already been carefully prequalified. Hence, when a need arises within a certain range of cost and effort, Edgar can immediately respond. On the other hand, without this prequalification background of Mary's instrumental value in the framework of Edgar's organized want system, it is unrealistic to assume the single thought "Mary needs help" to be sufficient to motivate Edgar to act. Of course, if the single thought "Mary needs help" of itself were sufficient to motivate Edgar to act, then Edgar must think of Mary's welfare as having a value that is more than a mere utility value *vis-a-vis* his own prioritized wants. But for Edgar to value the welfare of another without qualification, independent of the standard egoistic program, is for Edgar to be a normative agent who is no longer egoistic in my sense.

Many of the differences between the position I have developed on the egoist and the position Williams presents stems from differences in egoistic psychology. Whereas Williams discusses desires, whether of the egoist or of any other normative agent, as separate isolated springs to action, the desires of agent Edgar Egoist are conceptually intertwined with Edgar's concept of himself as an agent of a distinctive sort, whose fundamental normative principle gives unity to the on-going process of satisfying his desires in an organized and prioritized fashion. A psychology that attempts to capture the interplay of conceptual organization and desire is better equipped to handle the complexity of being an egoist, including accounting for the structure of his thought.

It may be objected that many selfish people or people with egoistic tendencies in real life appear to act on their desires in a disorganized and often spontaneous way, which may seem closer to the Williams' analysis of desire and motivation. However, most selfish people are simply confused about what they want and how to get it, and therefore provide a poor model of consistency and efficiency in motivation and action. One must remember that I am trying to present the strongest possible case for the amoral egoistic option, an account that is as consistent as possible and one that retains the character of the genuine egoist. If many people fill their lives with inconsistency in a confused and ineffectual display of their selfishness, their numbers do not increase one iota their appeal as a normative model. On the contrary, the inconsistency and disorganization, however "realistic," diminishes both the clarity of the egoistic picture, as well as its appeal or attractiveness.

A FRAMEWORK FOR EVALUATING EDGAR'S APPEAL

With these important background discussions behind us, I now directly address the answering of the question "Why should I be moral rather than an Edgar Egoist?". In so doing, I will present a framework in which the appeal of an amoral personal egoist like Edgar can be evaluated. From the initial standpoint of the non-egoist, the question can be articulated in terms of considerations which contribute to or diminish the appeal of a way of life one does not share. From the initial standpoint of being an amoral personal egoist, the question can be articulated in terms of the advantages and disadvantages of remaining[14] an amoral egoist versus going with a life-entrenchment that is non-egoistic. In what follows, whether stated in terms of appeal or in terms of reasons for what I, any first person raiser of the question, should become or remain, the same question is at issue: Given the genuine practical alternative of being a sophisticated, dedicated and consistent amoral personal egoist, like Edgar, what considerations with what advantages and disadvantages need to be addressed?

For simply convenience of discussion I will divide these considerations into two sorts: theoretical and practical considerations.[15] I will address in turn the theoretical and then those practical matters which are involved in any serious and careful attempt to answer the question at issue. The argument that develops from this discussion will be the following: the life-entrenchment of an amoral personal egoist like Edgar involves paying considerable prices both in terms of theoretical limitations and assumptions and in terms of human costs. In short, the life of Edgar Egoist has systematically built into it both theoretical and practical considerations which drastically diminish its appeal.

In *A Theory of Reasons for Action* David Richards writes that for the Master Criminal it will be irrational for him to be moral because he can successfully profit from the morality of others "… without himself undergoing all the costs of being consistently moral in all cases."[16] In focusing on the theoretical problems and practical disadvantages of *systematically being an egoist*, I attend to Edgar's *costs of being consistently egoistic in all cases* while he is trying hard to avoid the more commonly recognized costs of being consistently moral in all cases.

The amoralist is sometimes considered as having "nothing to lose," no prices to be paid. In the following, I point out that the amoralist who is a personal egoist like Edgar may have considerable costs that systematically accrue from his program independent of his success in individual transactions with others. And even if Edgar wins all "battles" with his resource-obstacles within the life-style in which he has entrenched himself (he fools them all!), what are the costs of the continual entrenchment itself? The mercenary soldier who wins all battles but dies miserably alone in his trench has paid considerable costs although he has been maximally efficient within his limited plans. Edgar Egoist may avoid directly confronting questions about the systematic costs of his life-style, but the questions remain. A related critical question is whether Edgar treats himself as an end, a la his egoistic imperative, given the systematic consequences of egoistic entrenchment.

Before turning to specific kinds of systematic costs of being an Edgar Egoist, starting with the theoretical limitations, I will reconsider a key point made in A. I. Melden's important early article "Why Be Moral?" Melden argues that a question like "Why be moral?" is an impossible question to answer. Since only the commitment to morality itself can be a reason for being moral, to demand some other reason, where no other is possible, is due to a basic confusion. With the challenging amoralist, we have no theoretical issue, but only a practical problem of how to handle him.[17] According to Melden, to attempt to reduce or analyze the moral attitude in terms of an amoralist's reasons (that are void of moral considerations and moral attitude) is to confuse two different meanings of reasons. No theoretical issue is common because no common ground exists, according to Melden, on the key point of a common criterion for what is reasonable. For the moralist the reasonable is morally defined; for the amoralist it is not.

Now Melden is correct in saying that the amoralist provides no theoretical problem for us moralists *within* morality and its practices. Similarly, we moralists share with the amoralist no theoretical issue within morality, for the amoralist chooses to stay *outside* morality and the reach of its moral reasonableness. But not all theoretical issues must be issues within moral theory. In this concluding chapter, the theoretical problems I attribute to the life and thought of Edgar Egoist are not problems defined by non-egoistic theorists which are then forced on an amoral egoism where they do not fit. Rather these theoretical difficulties arise out of being an amoral egoist. Put differently, if Edgar Egoist is what he is and does what he must do to succeed, then these theoretical problems are present, whether or not an Edgar Egoist explicitly addresses them or not. One of the ways that my account of amoral personal egoism a la Edgar is different is that I provide for Edgar the sophistication, systematization, and complexity in which theoretical difficulties can occur, and therefore such problems can be recognized. My argument for my interpretation of Edgar Egoist's agency has been the following: If the agency of Edgar Egoist is to be both interesting and challenging in the spirit of Plato, and also not sloppy and inefficacious, but both systematic and reasonably consistent, then Edgar will think, organize, develop habits, and interact in such and such ways. The sophistication of Edgar's agency provides it with theoretical features, and therefore it has the potential for theoretical difficulties.

THEORETICAL DIFFICULTIES
BUILT INTO EDGAR'S AGENCY

One such potential difficulty for Edgar Egoist I label his *methodological isolationism*. This isolation arises from Edgar's attempt both to maintain systematically the egoistic integrity of his agency and to avoid slipping into the confusion and complications of inconsistency. A good question to ask, when an amoral egoist like Edgar attempts to avoid inconsistency by trying to evade or slide by all arguments regarding interpersonal justification, is where does the argument lead or, put differently, where do these problems resurface? I have discussed the difficulty of evaluating the thought of Edgar Egoist due to the non-egoist's overestimating the common ground that we (all non-egoists) share with Edgar. One might say that this lack of common ground has been an advantage that Edgar could wield when in a tough argumentative spot. However, the other side of this same coin is that this lack of common ground may be indicative of important limitations of his egoistic position.

In sharp contrast to Edgar, some philosophers of the practical life think of themselves as members of a core group of philosophers who approach the whole area of the normative, including the clarification and evaluation of language, reasoning and methods, with a view toward attaining the truth about morality. Such cognitivists hold that there is a normative truth to be known that is applicable to all human agents. Now an amoral personal egoist like Edgar does not participate in a serious way in this practice of philosophic truth-seeking about a common morality. Whatever the reason that Edgar does not participate in serious investigation about morality, whether he does not care to or whether he just wants to avoid inconsistency, the issue whether there is any point to such a practice of moral truth-seeking remains. The amoral egoist's failure to address this philosophical issue will not be a major factor in the valuation of egoistic attractiveness to the non-philosopher, but such theoretical incompleteness does matter to philosophers, who realize that, as a normative posture with theoretical content, Edgar's amoral personal egoism is subject to many of the same clarifying questions of theory as are other normative positions. Theoretical neglect or inactivity does not eliminate problems of theoretical clarity.

The theoretical incompleteness of Edgar's methodological isolationalism is again problematic if one traces his reason-having practices back to his fundamental egoistic principle and *agent-anschauung*. As I have discussed, Edgar Egoist's reason-having judgments, rules, and practices systematically reduce to his prioritized wants and his fundamental amorally egoistic agency itself. So that if one were to ask, "Well, why be amorally egoistic at bottom?" Edgar could reply, "... because I have so decided to be that sort of agent." Of course, in taking this sort of Aiken-like metaethical approach to any scrutiny of his ultimate entrenchment, Edgar has accomplished both maintaining the uniqueness of his agency (and does not resort to some form of utilitarianism, for example) and also minimizing the opportunity for falling into consistency problems. On the other hand, the question arises for Edgar, whether he carefully attends to it or not: Why accept this theoretical assumption, that Edgar's ultimate "decision" on his unique agency is not open to philosophic criticism, and that his "decision" is untethered to any other assumption which may itself be open to philosophic criticism?

The short of the matter is this. Edgar Egoist can methodologically isolate himself from much possible criticism, especially that his posture is not genuinely egoistic and/or that his posture is not consistent. However, the theoretical assumptions upon which this systematic avoidance and "ultimate" decision are dependent still remain, and the philosophic acceptability and criticism of same are open to question, whether an agent like Edgar in practice attends to them or not.[18]

Another theoretical question arises problematically out of Edgar's systematic isolationalism. This question is whether Edgar has taken some metaphysical baggage in with him into the "safe harbor" of his methodologically isolationary stance. Or put differently, is it possible for the amoral egoist to effectively insulate himself from all metaphysical discussion, by declining to do metaphysics just as he refuses to prescribe for all or justify to others? It is interesting to note that it is necessary for Edgar to maintain complete normative and procedural control in order to both avoid inconsistency and maintain his normative secrecy; hence, the need for discipline in his religiously careful illocutionary practices, in the prioritization of his wants, and in the application of his egoistic imperative.

But there is an important metaphysical assumption that must be made by Edgar to keep his control of all the shots within his little isolated cocoon of normative agency. Edgar assumes God does not exist, that there is no "searcher of hearts." This assumption that God does not exist is necessary for the maintenance of theoretical integrity of Edgar's amoral egoism because, if there exists a "searcher of hearts," then Edgar's normative game with all its home court advantages is not the only game in town. In fact, we then have a system within a system, Edgar's made-to-order normative system over which he wants complete control within an on-going system of normative evaluation, within which larger system his egoistic control and entire program is subject to a very non-egoistic evaluation. In short, the larger theoretical package of amoral egoism carries with it an important atheological base, and hence, at least one important metaphysical assumption.[19]

HUMAN COSTS OF
SYSTEMATICALLY BEING LIKE EDGAR

I turn now from these theoretical considerations to practical ones, from the limitations of Edgar's theory to the practical disadvantages or human costs of being an amoral personal egoist like Edgar. My argument has been that the question "Why should I be moral?" is a genuine question of practical importance; that the key to understanding that practical importance is to understand that practical alternative of being an amoral personal egoist. I have then argued that, if my description of such an agency is to be both genuinely amoral and egoistic, and therefore challengingly interesting to ethics, as well as to remain reasonably consistent and not self-defeating, then this Edgar Egoist agent must be described with such and such features of organization, principle, and habit formation. In the remainder of this chapter, I consider the different human costs or consequences of being entrenched in a life so described.

The first human cost or practical consideration for a normative agent like Edgar Egoist is that such a life is simply a hard or difficult life. How difficult a life will depend upon Edgar's particular set of prioritized wants. But the difficulty is *systematically* far reaching because of Edgar's need to simultaneously juggle (a) society's norms and social consequences, (b) Edgar's own egoistic program, and (c) the normative guidance of proximate resource persons like son Egbert under a careful disguise of intentions. I say that Edgar's life is systematically more difficult because the careful application of his egoistic system requires the continual application of this three-step evaluation process. Now what is more difficult about Edgar's evaluation program as compared with that of Mike Moralist is (1) the need for secrecy of agency identification and (2) the fact that for Edgar (a), (b), and (c) evaluation needs above are always active and never nearly reducible to one another.

For Mike Moralist, his own moral principles (corresponding to [b] for Edgar) will be slightly different than society's norms due to his own independent moral beliefs and principles, but the application of his moral principles only becomes problematic when the moral principles (b) are at variance with society's norms (a). For Edgar, his concealed egoistic proram (b) is in principle a different program than (a) and therefore demands a continual and independent evaluation process. Furthermore, in passing the baton of morality to his daughter Maureen, Mike Moralist will pass a program (c) to Maureen that is the same or nearly the same as Mike's (b). With Edgar's attempt to help build a set of principles for his son Egbert, Edgar must proceed carefully all the while concealing the nature of (b) while encouraging in Egbert a (c) set of principles and habits that are maximally efficient in their instrumentality for assisting Edgar in fulfilling his own secret egoistic program. In short, the egoistic system of Edgar Egoist necessarily involves a complex multi-layer of normative evaluation that is more difficult[20] to apply. Such day-to-day complexity, and its costs in terms of stress and energy expenditure, must be weighed against any apparent goals of the entire egoistic program.

The second consideration I turn to raises the question whether by carrying out the egoistic program Edgar himself thereby systematically places obstacles to his own personal happiness. In particular, I have in mind Joseph Butler's writing on immoderate self-love and the necessity of disengagement for personal enjoyment.

Immoderate self-love does very ill consult its own interest: and, how much soever a paradox it may appear, it is certainly true, that even from self-love we should endeavour to get over all inordinate regard to, and consideration of ourselves.[21]

The question or challenge for Edgar Egoist is whether his egoism with its conceptual organization and *agent-anschauung* is systematically inclined toward immoderate and, therefore, self-defeating desire for one's own personal happiness. To avoid such self-defeating immoderate concern for self, Edgar Egoist, as I have described him, must use rules of thumb and constitutive egoistic rules to avoid conveying to his obstacle-resource people (all others) any clumsy anxiety or blatant selfish behavior which will be counterproductive in bringing about the satisfaction of his prioritized wants, with the help of these others.

But it is one thing to fool others and be socially efficient with others, it is another to be able to psychologically handle *oneself* and not to systematically place psychological obstacles in one's own way. Again Joseph Butler reminds us,

Disengagement is absolutely necessary to enjoyment: and a person may have so steady and fixed an eye upon his own interest, whatever he places it in, as may hinder him from *attending* to many gratifications within his reach, which others have their minds *free* and *open* to.[22]

The challenge for Edgar Egoist is whether he can attain some sort of disengagement from his own secret egoistic planning through the time-outs of egoistic rules in designated social situations and personally calculated periods of rest and recreation.

The chief problem is whether Edgar can ever really get psychologically free for certain kinds of enjoyment when the egoistic override is always applicable and the need for special egoistic planning is a constant battle in which the egoist must be continually prepared for nimble changes as events and persons change his estimate of alternative consequences. The greater challenge is not with the threat of immoderate desire and inefficient behavior because, as I have defined Edgar, this sort of egoist can be self-disciplined enough to efficiently refine his wants and methods and also to restrain self-defeating desires. However, the greater challenge for Edgar is with engagement, whether he has systematically placed too great a psychological burden on himself leaving no or little possibility for the psychological freedom to disengage from the program to enjoy anything other than the egoistic puzzle working.

In the remainder of this chapter I will discuss those satisfactions, enjoyments or important human experiences that are distinctly absent from the life of an Edgar Egoist. I begin with the writing of Henry Sidgwick who eloquently notes several kinds and degrees of enjoyment that Edgar may fall short on:

> ... on empirical grounds alone, enlightened self-interest would direct most men to foster and develop their sympathetic susceptibilities to a greater extent than is now commonly attained. The effectiveness of Butler's famous argument against the vulgar antithesis between Self-love and Benevolence is undeniable: and it seems scarcely extravagant to say that, amid all the profuse waste of the means of happiness which men commit, there is no imprudence more flagrant than that of Selfishness in the ordinary sense of the term—that excessive concentration of attention on the individual's own happiness which renders it impossible for him to feel any strong interest in the pleasures and pains of others. The perpetual prominence of self that hence results tends to deprive all enjoyments of their keenness and zest, and produce rapid satiety and *ennui*: the selfish man misses the sense of elevation and enlargement given by wide interests; he misses the more secure and serene satisfaction that attends continually on activities directed towards ends more stable in prospect than an individual's happiness can be; he misses the peculiar rich sweetness, depending upon a sort of complex reverberation of sympathy, which is always found in services rendered to those whom we love and who are grateful. He is made to feel in a thousand various ways, according to the degree of refinement which his nature has attained, the discord between the rhythms of his own life and of that larger life of which his own is but an insignificant fraction.[23]

Now, as I have discussed, an enlightened egoist like Edgar will refrain from crudely selfish behavior that will label or characterize him to his disadvantage. But the challenge for Edgar is whether his selfish-in-principle normative posture can avoid the loss of these enjoyments: whether Edgar can attain the psychological equivalent of genuine interest in other people. I do not see how he can; again Edgar may be able to fool others, but not himself.

In pointing out these human costs of such an egoistic posture toward life and other people, I realize that an agent like Edgar may not admit the experiences that he misses as having much significance, or that he may judge these "human costs" are a bargain price that he can afford to pay, given his prioritized wants. If so, it is appropriate to point out Edgar's ignorance or his being "blind" to considerable human enjoyments. Of course, judging on issues of practical truth, and who is blind or ignorant, is like the question "Why should I be moral?" itself, right at the cutting edge of first-person acceptability. Even though Edgar may not want or have to articulate interesting differences with Sidgwick on what he may be missing, still, these considerations remain part of any careful checklist regarding the human costs of being an Edgar Egoist.

Before examining Edgar's capacity for friendship and love, I focus upon an important psychological need, the satisfaction of which is systematically ruled out by Edgar's program. I call it the problem of *psychological identification*. Given Edgar's strategic need for secrecy about the nature of his agency, he cannot share *who he really is* with any other human person. Yes, Edgar can share some, or even many, of his wants with some other persons when it is tactically safe and efficient to do so *vis-a-vis* the steady application of his normative program. But whatever is shared about who he is must always fall short of disclosing that essential element of an accurate description, that he is an amoral personal egoist and what that means. Edgar can identify himself in the sense of understanding who he is and how he differs from other agents, but he cannot identify himself *to others* as to who he really is. This human need, to share with some other person who one is, I take to be a very strong need, and to give up the opportunity to satisfy this need is to pay a high price. A corollary of this sacrifice is that Edgar can never have a genuine confidant in his life.

Another significant human cost to consider in evaluating the appeal of the egoistic challenge to morality is the problem of the limitations of one's friendships and the absence of the best kind of friendship. Here we have an area of human experience that, since Aristotle, has been considered an important part of human happiness; and yet the experience of genuine friendship is ruled out from the start by Edgar Egoist's normative approach to all other human agents. I concur with Aristotle that, "Those who wish for their friends' good for their friends' sake are friends in the truest sense, since their attitude is determined by what their friends are and not by incidental considerations."[24] But, of course, for Edgar nothing is either planned for or acted upon for the sake of another person. All Edgar's so-called friends, whether they know it or not,[25] will be friends incidentally because of the utility or pleasure that Edgar accrues from the relationship. Regarding

Edgar's friendships of utility, Kant notes in his *Lectures on Ethics*, "The delight of friendship does not consist in the discovery that there is a shilling for me in a stranger's moneybox."[26] And, with respect to Edgar's friendships based on pleasure or mutual taste, Kant calls such a friendship a pseudo-friendship because, "It consists in the pleasure we derive from each other's company, and not from each other's happiness."[27] Kant emphasizes a view that I share, that "The finest sweets of friendship are its dispositions of good-will."[28] These finest enjoyments of friendship accrue from genuine dispositions mutually understood that the happiness of each is willed by the other, where "... there is no question here of any service, or of any demand ...,"[29] as a condition for those dispositions. In short, "the finest sweets" of genuine friendship are systematically excluded from Edgar's program.

Like his handling of friendship, the lack of a role for genuine human love in Edgar's life and program is significant in any evaluation of the egoistic challenge to morality. For a discussion of love, I lean heavily on the work of Irving Singer.[30] I believe his account that follows to be basically correct. In the first chapter of his classic work, Singer defines love as an act and product of the imagination that creates a new value, a bestowal value. Singer contrasts the lover's bestowed value, which the lover gives to the beloved, to an "individual appraisal." The latter appraisal involves a deciding about what something (e.g., a house) is worth to *oneself*. Singer explains that a professional appraiser of houses will attempt to place an "objective value" that is verifiable in terms of features that fulfill specifiable criteria in a given market place of prospective buyers. However, the individual who is house hunting, although he will need at least a rough idea of what other buyers will pay (the objective value), will engage also in his own individual appraisal. In the latter the prospective buyer "... has to weigh, and so appraise, the relative importance of his own particular interests; and he must estimate whether the house can satisfy them."[31]

Singer then goes on to contrast both individual appraisal value and objective value with *bestowed value*, the key to his account of human love. The former, individual and objective value, depend upon an object's ability to satisfy prior interests, whatever needs or wants which motivate us toward one object rather than another.

Bestowed value is different. It is created by the affirmative relationship *itself*, by the very act of responding favorably, giving an object emotional and pervasive importance regardless of its capacity to satisfy interests.[32]

Singer points out that people, as well as houses, are also appraised, that in all communities, we constantly evaluate one another on the basis of our individual interests. Although sometimes very subtly, we are always setting prices on other people, and on ourselves in terms of each other's satisfactions.

Singer argues, however, that in bestowing value in the manner of love the bestowal valuing is importantly different.

> We then respond to another as something that cannot be reduced to *any* system of appraisal. The lover takes an interest in the beloved as a *person*, and not merely as a commodity (which she may also be). He bestows importance upon *her* needs and *her* desires, even when they do not further the satisfaction of his own. Whatever her personality, he gives it a value it would not have apart from his loving attitude. In relation to him, this woman has become valuable for her own sake.
>
> In the love of persons, then, people bestow value upon one another over and above their individual or objective value .... The lover makes the beloved valuable merely by attaching himself to her. Though she may satisfy his needs, he refuses to use her as a mere instrument. To love a woman as a person is to desire her for the sake of values that appraisal might discover, and yet to place one's desire within a context that affirms her importance regardless of these values. Eventually, the beloved may no longer matter to us as one who is useful. Treating her as an end, we may think only of how we can be useful to *her*. But still it is we who think and act and make this affirmative response. Only in relation to *our* bestowal does another person enjoy the kind of value that love creates.[33]

Singer goes on to say that love differs from related attitudes, like generosity or gratitude, in bestowing value without calculation.

My last argument, that Edgar Egoist misses out on human love in the fullest sense, can be summarized simply as follows: Edgar Egoist, as I have described him, never treats any other person, even his son Egbert, as an end in himself, as having a value in himself, independent of Edgar's egoistic schemes and utility calculations. While Edgar may pretend he is a lover a la Singer, by definition he is systematically limited to being an appraiser of resources, in which all other persons, like houses and wheelbarrows, are valued solely in terms of their utility within Edgar's egoistic program. To use Kant's terminology, like that of friendship, "the finest sweets" of being a genuine lover are systematically beyond Edgar's reach, as long as he remains entrenched in the amoral egoistic way of life.

SUMMARY AND LOOK AHEAD

In summary, I have argued that once one has adequately clarified the fundamental first-person acceptability question, "Why should I be moral rather than an amoral personal egoist (like Edgar), one arrives *not* at a single moment of arbitrary decision, that is free of all philosophic evaluation; rather one arrives at life's continually relevant, fundamental alternatives, alternatives which face a complex set of related philosophic assumptions, as well as the practical realities of the consequences of these alternatives.

I have then argued that the amorally egoistic agency of Edgar Egoist is fraught with theoretical liabilities and drastic human costs. On the theoretical side, Edgar's normative position is shackled with methodological isolationalism and is limited by the metaphysical assumption of atheism. On the practical side, a life-entrenchment like Edgar's systematically builds into its agency practical problems and systematically rules out important human experiences and sources of satisfaction and enjoyment. Confronting the personal egoist are the costs of additional stress and energy expenditures in handling his day-to-day multi-level evaluation program; and the continual price of not satisfying his need for psychologically identifying himself and the nature of his agency to others is a considerable price. In addition, I have questioned whether Edgar's egoistic system, whose complexity is necessary for his egoistic success and his consistency, allows him the freedom to disengage and enjoy anything more from life than the egoistic puzzle-solving that he must engage in as long as he remains an amoral personal egoist. And, I have argued that the agency of Edgar Egoist pays the enormous price of systematically ruling out the possibility of genuine human friendship and love for other people. Therefore, regarding first-person acceptability from the starting point of the non-egoist, the appeal of this sort of agency has been greatly diminished.

The *form of my argument* throughout has been the following. A description can be given of a normative agency that challenges morality in two ways, insofar as such an agent is both amoral and exclusively egoistic. As such, this agency is a genuine practical alternative to being moral. However, I have argued, if this sort of agent is to be both interesting and realistically efficient, then such an agency will have certain features. In the first place, such an amoral egoist must be a personal egoist: any other form of egoism is either not a serious normative entrenchment or is not at bottom a genuinely egoistic position. Second, to clarify properly the genuine alternative of Edgar's agency, I argued that one must look beyond behavior conformity, and one must articulate enough egoistic psychology to account for how an Edgar Egoist would organize his thinking and plan his strategy for dealing with human resources. Making use of my description of what Edgar's conceptual organization and social planning would be like, I enlarged on this to provide an account of how Edgar would use normative language and give reasons to other persons in a way that is internally consistent. And in this last chapter I have taken this agent, so described for the above reasons, and I have pressed the question, "... at what price?" My answer has been to lay out an important set of theoretical liabilities and practical costs for systematically being an Edgar Egoist.

In Chapter Four, when I evaluated Kai Nielsen's argument against the life-option of egoism, I noted that Nielsen's argument was shackled by severe definitional limitations. At that time I suggested a revision to Nielsen's argument that I am now in a better position to fill in. The revised Nielsen argument is the following: given what being an amoral personal egoist actually consists in, the conceptual development and practical maintenance of such an agency is disastrous to personal happiness. Undoubtedly, a very strong case can be made for this revised argument, pursuing the argument down several or all of the above, briefly discussed practical avenues. However, I leave it to others or to myself at another time to make the strong case against amoral personal egoism, to judge as to what is the knockout blow, what point most diminishes the appeal to a non-egoist. If I err on the side of leniency, in not pouring it on Edgar Egoist, it is because my primary concern has been to drive the question as far down the road of clarity as possible, in the spirit of Henry Sidgwick,[34] and to carefully lay out a balanced account of relevant considerations for first-person acceptability.

After all, the problem with philosophic attempts to evaluate the amoral egoist has not been due to a lack of desire or commitment to "put him away"; rather the problem has been the lack of a careful initial description of the interestingly complex amorally egoistic agency. As I see it, simplistic accounts of the amoral egoist have encouraged incomplete and superficial answers to the question, "Why should I be moral?" These accounts have still left the most interesting version of the question unattended to and therefore unanswered.

My primary contribution has been to provide the detailed characterization of amoral personal egoism that reveals this fundamental life-option as a real challenge to all moral points of view, an amoral egoism that has interest, involves commitment and is not simply the product of a confused and undisciplined mind. With my more promising description of the purely egoistic character in place, one can no longer talk so easily about an arbitrary "choice" that makes no difference *within* philosophy. One finds the option of Edgar's agency a package deal loaded with issues of theory and practice. And this package deal comes at considerable cost, the figuring of which is philosophically interesting.

As a check on my analysis and argument, one might query: Are these the results that one would expect from seriously pushing the title question? I respond with a short list of key characteristics of my analysis along with some common sense comments.

(1) The title question remains after my analysis still a *hard question* deserving of philosophic attention. In light of the history of philosophic discussion of Plato's challenge, I would seriously suspect fundamental flaws in my analysis and argument if the question became too easy to answer.

(2) That my analysis reveals considerable *complexity* in this first-person acceptability question itself, and its answer, is to be expected, given that life itself is challenging and life's agents and characters interestingly complex.

(3) The need and urgency for *quality moral education* in the home and in our communities has not been diminished. This is not unexpected, unless one holds that *simple* arguments are enough to make people good. Naive assumptions that the egoist must be significantly, even completely, deficient either intellectually or emotionally only help to underestimate the importance and difficulty of the moral education challenge in a world of instant communication.

(4) That the amoral personal egoist cannot be *argumentatively "taken out" so easily* by appealing to language or by simple methodological moves or by simply moving around the "ethical pale" is not unexpected. J. A. Brunton has reminded us that it is the egoistic way of life that has earned its widespread detestation, not the egoist's lack of linguistic sophistication. That the egoist is never selective and disciplined and that she will always trip over simple linguistic and social obstacles, thereby revealing herself, is wishful and naive thinking.

(5) That the analysis of the title question and the discussion of its answer remains *within philosophic discourse* and not outside it, is also not unexpected. To claim that these matters are beyond the realm of philosophic discussion and critique is a clarion call to the Glaucons of the world. Indeed, it would be strange if philosophy began to say nothing about such important matters, or better stated, it would be strange if all individual philosophers gave up on all argumentation at this fundamental level,[35] especially strange in this case with a question so practically important yet in such need for language analysis, consistency challenges and the recognition of metaphysical assumptions.

I have refered to the classic line of Brian Medlin, "I'm a philosopher, not a rat-catcher, and I don't see it as my job to dig vermin out of such burrows as individual egoism."[36] Leaving the vermin to move on his own, I have focused upon throwing light down the egoist's neglected burrow, taking a fresh look at his living conditions and finding philosophic questions entwined about his theoretical furniture. Unimpressed by the assumption that the egoist must be pampered on the sidelines, by expanding on his organization, language-use and reasoning, I have thrust the egoist into the arena of ethical discussion and raised questions about prices paid on the long-term installment plan for his systematic life style. I consider my efforts a service, not only for fellow Glaucon-types, but also for all those on both sides of the egoist-moralist chasm who are simply looking for greener grass.

Notes

1 Taylor, *Principles of Ethics*, pp. 226-27.

2 Henry David Aiken, *Reason and Conduct* (New York: Alfred A. Knopf, 1962), p. 86.

3   Regarding the talk about deciding to be moral or egoistic, Rodger Beehler (*Analysis*, 1972, see especially pp. 15-16) has seriously questioned whether this is the kind of thing one can decide. He asks, can you decide to have a regard for goodness, can you decide to care? Beehler is certainly correct in emphasizing the need for preparing the dispositions for caring or other virtuous activity. It is also true that the ordinary person cannot just decide at time t to care when she is very much not so disposed. But it may be possible in special circumstances to so decide to care, e.g. Paul on the road to Damascus.

But there is more to the complexity of "deciding" to be moral than just being disposed to care. Just as it makes very good sense to try to answer the also difficult question "why should I teach my children to be morally good persons?," it makes perfectly good sense to try to answer why should I be moral, including the related question why should I prepare myself such that I can be disposed to care for others, etc. To imply that questions like "why should I be moral?" are without point because it all depends on how one happens to care is to make a methodological move that drops some important questions (which will not go away) off the argumentative table without sufficient justification. Compare the above caring-response about the first-person question with the similar judgment that there is no point in my teaching my children to be moral because it will all depend upon whether they learn to care or not for others. Part of my answering the question what I should teach my children will involve whether and how I should prepare them to care, etc. Similarly, the whole point of trying to answer whether I should be moral involves whether there is point to *preparing* for caring for others, etc, or whether I should scrap the whole project and just work on preparing myself for the using-people project. See also Kai Nielsen's reply to Beehler in the same volume.

4   Murdoch, "Vision and Choice," p. 33.

5   Ibid., pp. 40-41.

6   Aiken, *Reason and Conduct*, p. 87.

7   Although I pursue the more fruitful question "Why should I *be* anything?", the question "Why should I *do* anything?" is not a senseless, "beyond reason" question. One sensible answer to the latter question is that I should eat something nutritious within the next 48 hours so that I do not collapse. I owe this argument to my colleague Harold Austin.

8   Bernard Williams, *Morality: An Introduction to Ethics* (New York: Harper & Row, 1972), p. 8.

9   Williams, *Problems of the Self*, p. 251.

10 Of course, the definition here is crucial in any claim to throw the egoist onto the psychopathic heap. If the psychopath is defined as unstable, as emotionally and behaviorally disordered, such descriptions do not capture, need not describe, Edgar Egoist.

It is true that the egoist does not perceive *in some sense* her social and moral obligations, at least not in the same way that the moralist sees them. But Edgar can learn conventional morality and understand very well what elements of conventional morality apply in what situations, i.e. what is required by conventional morality, as well as what are the consequences for noncompliance. Edgar's prudentially careful, *selective* moves of immorality are designed to avoid the appearance of antisocial behavior. For Edgar the normal patterns of description of the psychopathic individual are characterizations he definitely wants to avoid, again for Edgar, he likes it best when he can make maximal use of his human resources. Generic psychopathic behavior is self-defeating and a poor setup for future moves.

11 Ibid., pp. 260-61.

12 Ibid., p. 265.

13 Williams, *Morality*, p. 10.

14 As has been noted, a sloppy, inconsistent egoist can also raise the question whether he should make the commitment to become a serious, disciplined, and consistent egoist like Edgar.

15 I emphasize the convenience factor in making this distinction because in actual normative life the two are intertwined; one example of this interplay is Edgar Egoist's set of theoretical assumptions behind his practical life, which I discuss below.

16 David Richards, *A Theory of Reasons for Action* (Oxford, Oxford University Press, 1971), p. 271.

17 Melden, "Why Be Moral?" esp. pp. 455-56.

18 John Hospers writes that the personal egoist would not likely engage in philosophic discussion because "... It would hardly be to his interest to allow others to plant in his mind the seeds of skepticism concerning his egoistic doctrine." In "Baier and Medlin," p. 12.

19 One could come to Edgar's defense here and claim that Edgar need not be an atheist but can claim that he is an agnostic, that God may exist but Edgar just cannot know whether he does or not, and he is wagering his life, unlike Pascal, that God does not exist. While this argumentative move may have some advantages, it certainly does not simplify Edgar's position regarding

metaphysical and epistemological assumptions. Besides the interesting questions about the wager argument, all kinds of questions regarding what Edgar can know and human knowledge in general come to the fore.

20 Perhaps the most realistic approach to any study of just how much more difficult the life of Edgar Egoist would be is to focus on lives of espionage, for Edgar is an extreme case of a life of secrecy and deceit.

21 Butler, "Sermons and Dissertation Upon Virtue," Sermon XI, in *British Moralists*, ed. L. A. Selby-Bigge (New York: Bobbs-Merrill Co., 1964), p. 230.

22 Ibid.

23 Sidgwick, *Methods of Ethics*, p. 501.

24 Aristotle, *Nicomachean Ethics*, Bk. VIII, 1156b, 9-11 (New York: Bobbs-Merrill Co., 1962), pp. 219-20.

25 Of course, Edgar's "friends" will be better resource persons if they believe they are friends of Edgar in the truest sense, and not merely because of their usefulness or pleasure-producing qualities. Edgar's challenge is to encourage and maintain these mistaken beliefs in his resource persons.

26 Immanuel Kant, *Lectures on Ethics*, trans. Louis Infield (New York: Harper & Row, 1963), p. 204.

27 Ibid., p. 205.

28 Ibid., p. 204.

29 Ibid., p. 205.

30 Irving Singer, *The Nature of Love: Plato to Luther* (New York: Random House, 1966).

31 Ibid., p. 4.

32 Ibid., p. 5.

33 Ibid., pp. 6-7.

34 For Sidgwick's stated attempt to seek maximal clarity on controversial questions, see his last paragraph of chapter one: "My object, then, in the present work, is to expound as clearly and as fully as my limits will allow the different methods of Ethics that I find implicit in our common moral reasoning; to point out their mutual relations; and where they seem to conflict, to define the issue as much as possible .... I have wished to keep the reader's attention throughout directed to the processes rather than the

results of ethical thought; and have therefore never stated as my own any positive practical conclusions unless by way of illustration: and have never ventured to decide dogmatically any controverted points, except where the controversy seemed to arise from want of precision or clearness in the definition of principles, or want of consistency in reasoning." *Methods of Ethics*, p. 14.

35 Of course, that large numbers of individual philosophers have neglected or given up on a question has been common to some very important questions in the history of philosophy.

36 Medlin, "Ultimate Principles and Ethical Egoism," p. 59.

Bibliography Of Works Cited

Aiken, Henry David. *Reason and Conduct*. New York: Alfred A. Knopf, 1962.

Annas, Julia. *An Introduction to Plato's Republic*. Oxford: Clarendon Press, 1981.

Anscombe, Elizabeth. "Modern Moral Philosophy." In *Ethics*, ed. Judith J. Thomson and Gerald Dworkin, 186-210. New York: Harper & Row, 1968.

Aristotle. *Nicomachean Ethics*. Trans. Martin Ostwald. New York: Bobbs-Merrill, 1962.

Baier, Kurt. "Rationality, Reason, and the Good." In *Morality, Reason and Truth*, ed. David Copp and David Zimmerman, 193-211. Totowa, N.J.: Rowman and Allanheld, 1985.

_____. "The Conceptual Link Between Morality and Rationality." *Nous* 7 (1982).

_____. *The Moral Point of View: A Rational Basis of Ethics*. Abridged ed. New York: Random House, 1965.

Beehler, Rodger. "Reasons For Being Moral." *Analysis* (1972): 12-16.

Bradley, F. H. "Why Should I Be Moral?" In *Ethical Studies* (Selected Essays), 3-28. New York: Liberal Arts Press, 1951.

Broad, C. D. "Certain Features in Moore's Ethical Doctrines." In *The Philosopy of G. E. Moore*, ed. P. A. Schilpp, 2nd ed., 43-57. New York: Tudor Publishing Co., 1952.

Brunton, J. A. "The Devil Is Not a Fool or Egoism Re-Visited." *American Philosophical Quarterly* 12 (1975): 321-30.

_____. "Egoism and Morality." In *Contemporary Ethical Theory*, ed. Joseph Margolis, 280-300. New York: Random House, 1966.

_____. "Restricted Moralities." *Philosophy* 41 (1966): 113-25.

Butler, Joseph. "Sermons and Dissertation upon Virtue." In *British Moralists,* ed. L. A. Selby-Bigge, 181-254. Indianapolis: Bobbs-Merrill, 1964.

Carlson, George R. "Ethical Egoism Reconsidered." *American Philosophical Quarterly* 10 (1973): 25-33.

Frankena, William K. *Ethics.* Englewood Cliffs, N.J.: Prentice-Hall, 1963.

Gauthier, David P., ed. *Morality and Rational Self-Interest.* Englewood Cliffs, N.J.: Prentice Hall, 1970.

Gert, Bernard. *Morality: A New Justification of the Moral Rules.* New York: Oxford University Press, 1989.

Gewirth, Alan. "Must One Play the Moral Language Game?" *American Philosophical Quarterly* 7 (1970): 107-18.

_____. "The Non-Trivializability of Universalizability." *Australasian Journal of Philosophy* 47 (1969): 123-31.

_____. *Reason and Morality.* Chicago: University of Chicago Press, 1978.

_____. "Replies to My Critics." In *Gewirth's Ethical Rationalism,* ed. Edward Regis Jr., 192-255. Chicago: University of Chicago Press, 1984.

Hare, R. M. *Freedom and Reason.* New York: Oxford University Press, 1965.

_____. *Moral Thinking.* Oxford: Clarendon Press, 1981.

Hospers, John. "Baier and Medlin on Ethical Egoism." *Philosophical Studies* 12 (1961): 10-16.

_____. *Human Conduct: An Introduction to the Problems of Ethics.* New York: Harcourt, Brace & World, 1961.

Irwin, Terence. *Plato's Moral Theory: The Early and Middle Dialogues.* Oxford: Clarendon Press, 1977.

Kalin, Jesse. "In Defense of Egoism." In *Morality and Rational Self-Interest*, ed. David P. Gauthier, 64-87. Englewood Cliffs, N.J.: Prentice-Hall, 1970.

_____. "On Ethical Egoism." *American Philosophical Quarterly*, Monograph Series 1 (1968): 26-41.

_____. "Public Pursuit and Private Escape: The Persistence of Egoism." In *Gewirth's Ethical Rationalism*, ed. Edward Regis Jr., 128-46. Chicago: University of Chicago Press, 1984.

_____. "Two Kinds of Moral Reasoning: Ethical Egoism as a Moral Theory." *Canadian Journal of Philosophy* 5 (1975): 323-56.

Kant, Immanuel. *Critique of Practical Reason*. Trans. Lewis White Beck. Indianapolis: Bobbs-Merrill, 1956.

_____. *Groundwork of the Metaphysic of Morals*. Trans. H. J. Paton. New York: Harper & Row, 1964.

_____. *Lectures on Ethics*. Trans. Louis Infield. New York: Harper & Row, 1963.

_____. *Religion Within the Limits of Reason Alone*. Trans. Theodore M. Greene and Hoyt H. Hudson. New York: Harper & Row, 1960.

Korsgaard, Christine. "The Sources of Normativity." Tanner Lectures, 1992, publication forthcoming by Cambridge University Press.

Kraut, Richard. "The Defense of Justice in Plato's *Republic*." In *The Cambridge Companion to Plato*, ed. Richard Kraut, 311-37. New York: Cambridge University Press, 1992.

Medlin, Brian. "Ultimate Principles and Ethical Egoism." In *Morality and Rational Self-Interest*, ed. David P. Gauthier, 56-63. Englewood Cliffs, N.J.: Prentice-Hall, 1970. Originally published in *Australasian Journal of Philosophy* 35 (1957), 111-118.

Melden, A. I. "Why Be Moral?" *The Journal of Philosophy* 45 (1948): 449-56.

Monro, D. H. *Empiricism and Ethics*. London: Cambridge University Press, 1967.

Moore, G. E. *Principia Ethica.* Cambridge: Cambridge University Press, 1903; paperback reprint ed., Cambridge: University Printing House, 1966.

Murdoch, Iris. "Vision and Choice in Morality." *Proceedings of the Aristotelian Society.* Supp. vol. 30 (1956): 32-58.

Nagel, Thomas. *The Possibility of Altruism.* Princeton, N.J.: Princeton University Press, 1970.

Nielsen, Kai. "Is 'Why Should I Be Moral' an Absurdity?" *Australasian Journal of Philosophy* 36 (1958): 25-32.

_____. "Morality and Commitment." In Nielsen's *Why Be Moral?*, 196-206. Buffalo, N.Y.: Prometheus Books, 1989.

_____. "Must the Immoralist Act Contrary to Reason." In *Why Be Moral?*, 269-83.

_____. "Point of Morality." In *Reason and Practice: A Modern Introduction to Philosophy*, ed. Kai Nielsen, 314-19. New York: Harper & Row, 1971.

_____. *Why Be Moral?* Buffalo, N.Y.: Prometheus Books, 1989.

_____. "Why Should I Be Moral?" In *Why Be Moral?*, 167-95.

_____. "Why Should I Be Moral?—Revisited." In *Why Be Moral?*, 284-300.

Plato. "Apology." In *The Last Days of Socrates*, ed. Hugh Tredennick, 45-76. Baltimore, Md.: Penguin Books, 1969.

_____. "Gorgias." In *The Collected Dialogues of Plato.*, ed. Edith Hamilton and Huntington Cairns, 230-307. New York: Bollingen Foundation, 1961.

Plato. *Republic.* Trans. G. M. A. Grube, revised by C. D. C. Reeve. Indianapolis: Hackett Publishing Co., Inc., 1992.

_____. *The Republic of Plato.* Trans. Francis M. Cornford. New York: Oxford University Press, 1945.

Popper, Karl R. *Conjectures and Refutations: The Growth of Scientific Knowledge.* New York: Harper & Row, 1968.

Prichard, H. A. "Duty and Interest." In *Readings in Ethical Theory*, ed. Wilfrid Sellars and John Hospers, 469-86. New York: Appleton-Century-Crofts, 1952.

Rawls, John. *A Theory of Justice*. Cambridge, Mass.: Harvard University Press, 1971.

Reeve, C. D. C. *Philosopher-Kings: The Argument of Plato's Republic*. Princeton: Princeton University Press, 1988.

Richards, David. *A Theory of Reasons for Action*. Oxford: Oxford University Press, 1971.

Sidgwick, Henry. *The Methods of Ethics*. 7th ed. Chicago: University of Chicago Press, 1907.

Singer, Irving. *The Nature of Love: Plato to Luther*. New York: Random House, 1966.

Smart, J. J. C. "Extreme and Restricted Utilitarianism." In *An Historical Introduction to Moral Philosophy*, ed. Michael F. Wagner, 215-20. Englewood Cliffs, N.J.: Prentice Hall, 1991.

Sprigge, T. L. S. "Definition of a Moral Judgment." In *The Definition of Morality*, ed. G. Wallace and A. D. M. Walker, 119-45. London: Methuen & Co., Ltd., 1970.

Taylor, Paul W. *Principles of Ethics: An Introduction*. Encino, Calif.: Dickenson Publishing Co., 1975.

Toulmin, Stephen. *An Examination of the Place of Reason in Ethics*. Cambridge: Cambridge University Press, 1964.

Wadia, P. S. "Why Should I Be Moral?" *Australasian Journal of Philosophy* 42 (1964): 216-26.

White, Nicholas P. *A Companion to Plato's Republic*. Indianapolis: Hackett Publishing Co., Inc., 1979.

Williams, Bernard. *Morality: An Introduction to Ethics*. New York: Harper & Row, 1972.

_____. *Problems of the Self*. Cambridge: Cambridge University Press, 1973.

Wittgenstein, Ludwig. *Philosophical Investigations*. Trans. G. E. M. Anscombe. New York: Macmillan Co., 1953.

Index